YOUNG POETS
of Central New Jersey

A collection of student poetry published in the Courier News

2005

Published by the Courier News, Bridgewater, N.J.

Copyright 2006 © Courier News.

All rights reserved. No portion of this book may be reproduced without the prior written consent of the Courier News.

DISCLAIMER: Poems in this book were submitted to the Courier News by students with a parent's approval. All submissions were accompanied by forms verifying that the poems are the students' original work and were not copied from another source.

Cover and interior design by Leeza Hernandez.

Edited by Courier News staff.

Library of Congress Cataloging-in-Publication Data: Pending

First Edition

Manufactured in the United States.

Genre: Poetry

ISBN 0-9772621-0-3

Published in the United States by the Courier News.

Registered domain: www.c-n.com

CONTENTS

Introduction i

1	Kindergarten	1
2	First Grade	7
3	Second Grade	11
4	Third Grade...	19
5	Fourth Grade.......................................	31
6	Fifth Grade..	43
7	Sixth Grade...	53
8	Seventh Grade....................................	69
9	Eighth Grade	117
10	Ninth Grade..	135
11	Tenth Grade	143
12	Eleventh Grade...................................	153
13	Twelfth Grade.....................................	159
14	No Grade Given	163

Index 169

INTRODUCTION

Welcome to a world of young voices

How do young people see the world?

That's what we wondered. And that's what we found out.

In early 2005, the Courier News invited students from Central New Jersey to send us their poetry. We promised to publish at least one of the poems every day in our local news section.

The result was a flood of poems by students from the lowest grades up through high school. We are happy to reproduce here all the poems that ran in the newspaper. We have grouped the poems by the grade levels of the students.

Some of the images are happy ones. Some show the brooding side of adolescence. The poems show the range of emotions and ideas you would expect to find among dozens of young people.

How do they see the world?

Turn these pages and find out.

Charles W. Nutt,
Publisher, Courier News

Chapter 1
KINDERGARTEN

Young Poets of Central New Jersey

Snowman

Snow
Nose
Outside
Wintertime
Mom and dad
Arms
No legs

Bailey Tocci,
Warren

Smile

I smile when I see butterflies.
I smile because I love.
I smile at school.

Julia Sikora,
Mountainside

Apples

Are good to eat
I like them whole
They are hard to bite
And cold on my teeth

Ali Ahmed,
North Plainfield

My Favorite Things

My cats
Pretty hats
Drawing
Cats pawing
Nikko, my stuffed pet
Minx, the bunny I met

Emily DeSotelle,
North Plainfield

Untitled

My name is Aneesh Agrawal
I like soccer and kickball.
It's fun for me except when
it hits the mailbox.
Sometimes it looks like a baby fox.
My lion
Is afraid of water
It likes to hunt for zebra
Likes to see birds to eat
It's true

Aneesh Agrawal,
Branchburg

I Am An Artist

I am an artist
I like painting stuff
Like people and houses
Outside
I like drawing stuff like
People planting flowers
And singing
On microphones

Naomi Taylor,
North Plainfield

My Rhyming Words

I like to jump and run
It is a lot of fun
I like to jump in the sun
In the sun I like to run

I like to play with my bear
He has dark brown hair
I won him at the fair
I care about my bear

I like to draw different things
Flowers, butterflies and kings
I like to wear lots of rings
I like to wear my fairy wings

Elena Bermudez,
North Plainfield

Chapter 2
FIRST GRADE

Untitled

My hamster is small and fluffy.
She adores to race with me.
Hamtaro gets out of her cage at midnight.

Brandon Stoeckel,
Branchburg

History

I know about history,
I know about happy things,
I know about native Americans,
Lewis and Clark, Martin Luther
King Jr., and Rosa Parks.
I know about history,
There is a lot of history
and it could be anywhere you could be.
Presidents are in history, like
George Washington, and that's all I know.
There is one more thing I know...
It was a long time ago!

Danny Edman,
Watchung

My Dog

Diva, when you smell her,
She smells good,
If you feel her she's soft,
She can run faster than you,
Nobody can beat her,
No you can't
Diva is our dog and nobody can beat her

Tasha Bethea,
Piscataway

Chapter 3
SECOND GRADE

My Favorite Season

Spring is here.
It brings good cheer.
It's my favorite time of year.

Flowers bloom.
I see them from my room.
They chase away the gloom.

I love to run and play.
The sun is here to stay.
We'll have fun all day.

Birds fly through the sky.
I wish I could fly that high.
If I could, I'd say bye-bye.

Jennifer Johnson,
Middlesex

Hawks

Hawks hunting rodents,
Mice squeaking, rats running, swoop!
Hawks are getting food.

Connor Greig,
Flemington

Beach

Pretty hard shells,
Wiggly salt-water fish swim,
Eels hiding in sea.

Brandon Stein,
Flemington

Flowers

I like to look at Roses,
I like to look at Lilies
What would you do if you cut one or two?
I would put them in a vase,
I would put them on the table,
Then when my mother came
In she would know
That I am able to cut
Them for the table.

Melanie Nettler,
Westfield

You

Your eyes remind me of the riverbank swishing. Your face makes me feel like the wind blowing through my hair. When I'm around you I feel like a bird soaring softly into the sky. When I see you I feel like a butterfly in the wind.
Your picture in my room reminds me of a leprechaun sliding down his rainbow. When you go past me I feel a baby bird hatching in my hand.

Jessica Tobia,
Bridgewater

My Tiny Dog's Name Is Sam

My tiny dog's name is Sam,
and he is very nice,
Most of the time,
We give him rice.
Sam likes to eat people food,
When he does that ... he's in a great mood!
Sam's weight is about 20 pounds,
One time in the backyard,
A chicken bone was found!

Sam is really a good guard dog,
But sometimes he sits around like a boring log!
All I know is he loves me and I love him!

Garrett Szeto,
Fanwood

Nature

Nature is like rockets blasting off,
Nature is small when water zooms off.
Nature is leaves that fall on me,
Nature is trees that grow with me.
Nature is a stream that you can follow to happiness,
Nature is snow that brings joy to kids.
Nature is amazing,
Nature is beautiful,
Nature is everything that I love.

Vihar Desu,
Green Brook

Wacky Annie!

She likes to be called Bannie
When she thinks about that,
It tickles her funny bone
And then she begins to moan.

Sweet dog
Wish it was mine!
Always is so cute and cuddly
I can't wait to get one to keep.

Annie Yang,
Branchburg

Kimba's Mom

Once upon a time when the trees whispered
And when stars raced in the sky
One night the forest was silent and smoke filled the sky
And the stars were silent that night.

Kimba's mom saw that the stars grew still.
She saw some things in the distance.
Why did this strange creature come to our homeland?
What was its name?
Humans.

Humans are destroying our forests.
That night I will never forget.
When the humans came and the smoke filled the air
And the stars were silent.

Alexandra Lilly,
Martinsville

I Wish I Had A Dog

I wish I had a dog,
It's so much better than a frog.
I wish I had a frog,
It's so much better than a hedgehog.
I wish I had a hedgehog,
It's so much better than a hog.
I wish I had a hog, but what I
would really want is a dog!

Jeremy Algoo,
Green Brook

What Is Beautiful To Me

Above, above
Sunset is setting in the sky,
Below, below
Flowers are blooming from the ground.
In the mountains, the mountains,
Waterfalls are coming down really fast,
In the ocean, the ocean,
Dolphins are playing ball,
Here ends my song,
The beautiful world, Earth!

Samantha Todd,
Middlesex

Chapter 4
THIRD GRADE

The Changing Seasons

The Changing Seasons
Winter, Spring, Summer, Fall.
Winter is cold.
Spring is warm.
Summer is hot and last but not least,
Fall is nice and cool.
In winter it snows,
In spring it rains,
In summer the sun pops out and last but not least,
In fall all the beautiful leaves drop from the trees.
That is what I have to say about the changing seasons.

Shelby Sharkey,
Bridgewater

Outside

When I look outside at day
It is so shining bright
And it's so dark and gloomy outside at night.
In the day, the birds are chirping and flying with glee
They are an orchestra for you and me.
The flowers are blooming
Coming up like a tower
Let the rain shower
So the flowers stay alive
And that will bring glee to me.

Adam Murphy,
Raritan Borough

Spring Time

"Chirp, chirp, chirp,"
Plump robins,
Embark on their nesting.
The fiery sun,
Shining down,
On trivial,
Pink buds.
Snakes glissade,
Through the meadows,
That earned,
Their green.
Flowers receive,
Petals after coming up,
From the coco, brown dirt.
Bare trees,
Soon gain,
Their leaves.
Joyful kids,
Play under the never ending
Blue skies
Bright, white,
Cottony clouds,
Sail by.
Lakes glisten,
On the horizon,
As a beautiful sunny,
Spring day,
Vanishes.

Kristi Nichols,
Far Hills

The Quiet Place To Be

Sometimes I want to go to my secret place,
I go there without a trace,
Where I sit under a shaded tree,
What a sight to see,
Where the flowers smell like apples,
No one to bother me,
It sounds like the right place to be.

Branden Escott,
Middlesex

Love, Love ...

Love, love in the air,
Love, love everywhere,
Love, love in the mountain,
Love, love in the heart,
Love, love is in Cupid's arrow,
Love, love is not a game.
Love, love is sacred to couples,
Love, love is quite a feeling.

Nicolas Carra,
Raritan Borough

Butterflies

The most charming things in the world are butterflies.
They flutter around and around.
They are like little rainbows flying in the sky.
They are as small as a juice box.
When I am next to one I feel wonderful.

Thomas Healy,
Somerset

Animals After Hibernation

Sploosh!
Jumping in fervent water,
fish glisten.
Turtles slide,
out of shells.
Popping out of
dark burrows,
Fluffy bunnies
look around.
Brown salamanders cloak themselves
under rocks.
Buzz, buzz
Swarming bees.
Tired emerald caterpillars
Evolve into beautiful butterflies.
Engendering fortresses
strong ants do labor.
Possoms scavenge
for bugs
Proceeding out of dams
brown beavers build.
Black and white skunks
shift from hollow trees
to outside.
Zoom!
Flying in the sky
hawks plunge.
Birds return to
creative nests.
Mating gophers feast.
Sleepily groundhogs scurry
out of holes,
rapidly running
up trees.
Squirrels search for food.
Bugs slug out
of logs.

Sneaking out of under
tree stumps,
Petite mice
smell food.
Poom!
Black bats bolt
out of caves.
Scurrying out of
murky sewers
rats sniff.
Smart sly foxes
peek out of dens.
Lurching from
under logs sharp porcupines
defend themselves.
Dull moles excavate.
Coiling in ditches,
snakes slither.
Raccoons scamper out
of hollows.
Hibernation is done.
Next year,
Animals will,
Redo the process.

Kevin Wallace,
Bernardsville

The Months Of The Year

In January, I ski down a big, white mountain and can't see
what's coming around the next corner.
In February, it's Valentine's Day, a holiday that is full of love.
In March, Leprechauns dive into their pot of gold.
In April, my family and I celebrate Passover and hide the Matzo.
In May, daisies bloom in my back yard and I go to Hershey Park.
In June, school ends and I am excited about going to camp.
In July, I used to swim at my aunt's pool, but now I go to sleepaway camp.
In August, camp ends and then my family goes on vacation.
In September, school starts and I start a new grade.
In October, I dress up on Halloween and the trees' leaves fall off.
In November, my dad takes my sister and I to go vote.
In December, it's my birthday and there are lots of holidays.

Chloe Goldstein,
Warren

T. Rex Sue

Can the scientists find enough
DNA to recreate cool stuff?
They want to recreate the dinos
But so far found large groups of zeroes.
They found the fossil of T. Rex Sue
Her DNA was as good as glue.
So if they make a cloning machine
Will it bring back the T-Rex? She's mean!

Kathryn Northrop,
Bridgewater

I Have A Rocket

I have a rocket. I hide it in my pocket.
If it falls out, I will run all about!
I can't lose him. He's my best friend.

But I'm sorry this has to end.
I throw my rocket away so far
I think it almost hit a car.
I feel so sad
Even almost mad
When I find him I'll be happy.
When I see him I'll name him flappy.
I will have a rocket and
I will hide him in my pocket.

Yvonne Darlene Njoku,
North Plainfield

The Basilone Parade

Lots of sirens roaring.
Loud air horns blow.
Lots of loud people.
All very hot.
Everywhere you go is slow.
Everyone having fun.
People with balloon carts roam the streets.
Lots of people buying treats.
All firefighters very busy.
Cannons blowing.
Loud drums pounding.
Lots of fire trucks rolling.
All very tired.
Lots of Army people and things.
The streets are crowded and so are the sidewalks.
No place to go.
Everyone leaves after the parade is over.
The firefighters go to a firehouse and have lunch.
All are very tired and everyone is happy to get home and take a rest.
Two hours later the firefighters are home too. After that, everything is over.
Nothing else will happen until next year.

Danny Memoli,
Raritan Borough

Fishary

Deep, deep down, in the deep blue sea,
In the town of Fishary,
The only way to pay,
Was from the clay of Manta Ray.
The fish down there did not like that,
Especially Little Tatt.
Every morning, Little Tatt
and the other
members of Fishary,
Would go down and see Little Sam,
the mayor.
They would call him, "Little Sam,
Little Sam,"
and Little Sam would come out.
"Isn't there another way to pay,
Than from the clay of a Manta Ray?"
They would ask,
But Little Sam always replied,
"A law is a law,"
And with that, he would swim away.
The fish down there went on with that,
and Little Sam began to feel bad for Little Tatt,
He decided though, to keep that a secret.
So Little Tatt, and everyone saw Little Sam,
every day as usual.
For days, a week, a month.
Finally, Little Sam found what to pay with,
He phoned Little Tatt,
"Come to my office, now,"
He said, bring everyone in this town,
"I am sorry, I acted like a clown."
And everyone, they set off for Little Sam.
"And now," said Sam,
the only way to pay is from...
A CLAM!
Little Tatt thanked Little Sam,
And Little Sam, he said,

"Let's be friends."
So they were best friends,
from then on.
And they stayed paying with clams,
Until, they found something,
NEW!

Genevieve Cullen,
Warren

Imagination

A pretend world
I shut my eyes and imagine
The secret world in my head
It's there all the time
I think about it day and night
It's a thing everyone has

Justine Gray,
Bernardsville

Blue

Blue is a heron, a sapphire ring
The sound of the wind whistling in the air
Blue is the smell of swimming pools
The taste of chlorine
Blue is a warm blueberry pie
Sitting on the window sill
Blue tastes like cotton candy at the circus
Blue feels rough and cold
Blue is the color of flax and blueberries
Blue makes me feel comfortable!

Haley Fedak,
Glen Gardner

Chapter 5
FOURTH GRADE

My Brother Took My Homework

My brother took my homework,
he stuck it in his hair
When I turned him upside down,
my homework wasn't there
We looked in his shoe,
It smelled PU
but my homework wasn't there
We looked in his pockets,
but there were only rockets
but my homework wasn't there
We looked in his throat,
it smelled like a goat
but my homework wasn't there
My mom makes a fuss,
about missing the bus —
So I went on the bus without my homework

Adam Ludwigsen,
Bridgewater

Dream Lord

Wait till the Life
Wait till the Year,
Wait till the Month,
Wait till the Day,
Wait till the Hour,
Wait till the Minute,
Wait till the Second,
When the Dream Lord Comes to Grant Your Dream

Tara Manz,
Flemington

Life Is ...

Life is God's poetry book
with countless pages.
Every day, He reads a chapter.
He reads to himself
and His angels.
The pictures come to life.
God's poetry book
is a book filled with
Love and pain,
and all different cultures.
When you die He writes a
new poem in His Poetry Book.
Everyday,
God adds a chapter
To the book of
Love and Pain.
Life is like a fairy tale
with good endings, like
Living happily ever after.
and
Sad endings like a
Mother dying
leaving two children.
I wonder what
Fairytale ending
God has written for me.

*Crystal Myles,
South Plainfield*

Untitled

Fly away lies,
Honesty is here.
Stay away for good
And don't come near.
My mom doesn't like it,
Neither does my dad.
I can work on it,
And they surely will be glad!

Leah Agliata,
Hampton

Song Of The Unicorn

Like a spear,
Like a horn,
Like a spirit being born;

Like the hope of a child,
Like the wind in a storm,
I once have seen a unicorn;

Its horn tall and strong
His spirit as free as the wind,
Suddenly his pride drained,

I saw the ropes of the cowboy around his heart,
The village cried,
The cowboys cheered,

I felt a tear in my eye,
My heart broken,
I heard the wind sigh.

Ashley Thompson,
Hillsborough

My Grandma

My grandma was always nice and I loved her
even when we had fights
My grandma was always the boss
but she also made good pots of sauce
My grandma, she liked to play cards
but her favorite was to yell Bingo!
My grandma always gave me love
and I returned it with lots of hugs.
My grandma liked lots of people around
and in our house she never had a frown.
My grandma, now that we are apart
I want you to know you will always be in my heart.
My grandma, I'm here today to say this
You will always be missed.
Love,
Little Filippa

Filippa Primiero,
Bridgewater

Summer Time

In the nice and warm sun you see a bunny come.
The shadows the sway are the tall trees on a summer day.
The green grass as bright as green paint.
The flowers, blooming all around.
Fresh air fills your lungs.
The sky so bright and the clouds so white.
The one season enjoyed the most,
Summer.

Emily Butler,
Plainfield

On Grandma's Lap

On Grandma's lap I can hear
the needles banging together as she knits
a cozy rainbow quilt.
On Grandma's lap I can smell
nail polish as Grandma paints
her nails rosy red.
On Grandma's lap I can feel
Grandma rubbing my head
gently.
On Grandma's lap I can hear
her breathing calmly
when she kisses me on the cheek.
On Grandma's lap I can hear
her heart beating
very fast when I hug her close.
On Grandma's lap I can smell
sausage and peppers
baking in the kitchen.
On Grandma's lap I can hear
her singing a lullaby tenderly,
which makes me feel extra special inside.

Ashley Whitmore,
Warren

My Feelings

I feel sad some of the times,
But most of the times I'm happy like a clown.
When I'm sad I feel like hitting on somebody
When I'm sad I don't have much love for anyone
When I'm happy first I feel like I'm flying in the air.
Then when I'm sad I fall down and die.
My feelings are such a waste of time when I'm sad and mad.
So for you guys out there who are always sad or mad,
remember that those faces are ugly.

Taatiana Dixon,
Plainfield

I Wonder

I wonder if Dr. King is still alive
I wonder if Harriet Tubman has ever died
I wonder if my dad is really shy
I wonder if my mom has ever cried
I wonder if I'm a future boss
I wonder if my dad is Santa Claus
I wonder if I'm going to be a grown man
I wonder if I'll have five thousand fans
I wonder if five thousand blacks got away
I wonder if raining cats and dogs statement is true
I wonder why they call my little cousin Pooh
I wonder, I wonder, I wonder if it's blue and yellow thunder
That is what I wonder.

Najee Michael Lucky,
Plainfield

Dreams

Dreams are true.
Dreams do come true.
If anyone's dream comes true,
dream and your dream will come true too.
A dream is something that you
have to believe in.
Plus you can not give up.
Dreams are real.
Just believe in them all the time.
Dreams are something that can come true.
If you don't listen to other people.

Jamesetta Seebee,
Plainfield

Love

Love is in the air.
It's time that there is an affair.
We can love And there some one above.
We love each other, one more above us.
We can love or we can hate but we have to respect and appreciate
Love

Quajuan Mitchell,
Plainfield

Party

I'm on the roam
I'm talking on the phone
I'm going to a party
With a guy named Marty
Party like you just don't care
Throw your arms in the air
This is our freedom
Some one has the leadum
It's our right
To be cool and tight
We will party tonight

Alexis Koemm,
Somerville

A Pebble And A Waterfall

Falling, falling ...
Help!
Boulders fly by,
The waterfall is pulling me,
Down,
   Down,
      Down ...
Splash!
I hit the place below,
Ahh, calm water,
Circling around me, hugging me tight,
Saying "No more
waterfalls!"
I am a pebble
Woosh, woosh
I slash boulders,
Pick up pebbles,
Carry leaves —

Down, Down,
On my watery ride
Bumpety-bump!
Hitting a boulder — I don't mind.
I fly, soar over it ...
And then it's all over.
I drop the pebbles, and leaves.
Then I continue down this calm river to ...
Another one.
I am a waterfall.

Shirley Wang,
Bridgewater

All On A Summer's Day

Crickets chirping
Dog walking
Tomatoes growing
Bees buzzing
Wind blowing
Cars passing
Butterflies flying
Planes blinking
Me thinking
Flag hanging
Train whistle blowing
Birds soaring
Spiders crawling
Siren wailing
People laughing
Motorcycle revving
Ball playing
Bike riding
All on a summer's day

Erin Brooke Sweney,
Hillsborough

Sweetly

Sweetly is the student's smile who is happy for quite awhile,
Sweetly are the birds singing in the summer's quiet soft breeze,
Sweetly is the chocolate cake sitting on the table very well baked,
Sweetly are the flowers' smell that make the earth good and well,
Sweetly is the baby's laugh that makes you happy and content,
Sweetly are the summer's days that bring joy in many ways,
Sweetly are the children laughing but the sweetest of all is my mother's gentle call.

Maureen Hoey,
Bridgewater

Chapter 6
FIFTH GRADE

The Jump

As I canter down the path
Nothing shall stop me,
Not even a three foot jump
I steady my pace,
Lift my front feet,
I hear the crowd cheer
As I clear

Ashlee Steinberg,
Hillsborough

Beautiful Bubbles

Beautiful Bubbles
Floating around in the air,
Blowing bubbles for all to share.
They are easy to pop,
Get them before they drop.
Bubbles are everywhere
Even in your hair!
Having lots of great fun,
Shining in the bright sun.

Kathryn Dooley,
Hillsborough

Snow Day

Friends are sledding, building snowmen,
Making Angels,
Snowball fighting — all getting pounded.
Not me ...
I'm grounded.

Zachary Salisbury-Battista,
Middlesex

Summer And A Week At The Beach

A week at Stone Harbor,
Is never a bore.
When it's high tide,
It's boogie board time.
In the morning when it's low tide,
I hop on my bike and go for a ride.
I ride to the point to find special things,
Like conchs, sand sharks and shells of all kinds.
Miniature golf at Stone Harbor is really a blast,
The ice cream at Springers makes the memories last.
The dinners are fun,
the seafood is fresh,
A week at Stone Harbor is really the best!

Kimberly Kornbluth,
Bridgewater

Inside And Outside

Inside Park Middle School teachers are checking homework.
Outside spring is coming like a jet plane flying closer
and closer to New Jersey.
Inside lockers are closing like mine fields.
Outside cars are moving as if you were pressing a fast forward button.
Inside brains are popping from an overload of knowledge.
Outside people are jogging miles for their health.
Inside people are sleeping like polar bears hibernating.
Outside families are having barbeques and picnics for family fun.
Inside kids are playing sports in gym.
Outside girls are shopping like there are sales everywhere.
Inside we are all saluting the flag.

Brandon Smithwrick,
Scotch Plains

I Am

I am kind and curious
I wonder how the stars twinkle at night
I hear angels singing every morning
I see the flowers turning into bright gardens
I want world peace
I am kind and curious.

I pretend I am sleeping on a cloud
I feel a kitten cuddling with me
I touch the sun
I worry when I will die
I cry when someone is gone
I am kind and curious

I understand that no one is perfect
I say, "Follow your dreams"
I dream of riding a star
I try to be my best every day
I hope everyone will love one another
I am kind and curious

Daniela Traina,
Hillsborough

Art Helps

Too many thoughts running through my head
Where should I go?
I remember a place that someone said.
Homework, school, pressure to do well
I'm stressed out!
How did this happen? To do so much. I can't tell.
Walk out the door and go down the street
I can't wait for the surprise!
Into the studio, there we'll meet
Down stroke, up stroke, all you have to think about
So calming, creating a masterpiece
Almost there, time ... who needs to count.
A sun so bright, it hurts my eyes
A smiling person, so happy to see
You can't fail, whoever tries
The happiness that art can bring,
This helps us a lot, can't you tell?
Endless possibilities, make anything!
When you feel pressured and you want to get away,
Come and paint, whatever you please!
Time flies by, you'll never know how long you'll stay!
Not too much thinking involved.
You don't need tons of talent
Maybe your problems will be solved!
So paint, draw, sketch, sculpt ... how ever you want,
You WILL feel better, in no time at all!

Cara McPhillips,
Bridgewater

Heartache And Drama

Heartache and drama
Craziness and trauma
I think of all the pain
It's driving me insane
Cheating whispering lying

People can't stop crying
Both enemies and friendship
They just cause hardships
Rumors and despair
These people are unfair
You being mad
Causes me to be sad
Tears continue to flow
They are talking about you behind your back
And you don't even know
Afraid and unsure
I can feel so insecure
Slowly trying to get by
As I try not to cry
Waking up each morning
Not wanting to leave my bed
Because all of these emotions
Keep rushing through my head

Sarah Walters,
Dunellen

I See A Rainbow Of People

I see fiery reds who are bravest at heart
I see purples with passion for music and art
I can see greens who can grow seeds of love
I see bright shining yellows like stars from above
I see oranges better on a dull day
They do contrast deeply with shy, quiet gray
I can see blue, graceful and cool
I see a white that is softer than wool
But though there are all of these people I see
What do rainbow people see within me?

Sarah Antony,
North Plainfield

My Beginning

I was born high from heaven above
The clouds were holding me,
The sign of true love
I was soaring high in the sky
To the angels,
I had to say goodbye
I drifted down, earth so near
I loved the sounds that I could hear
I could hear the sound of a tiger stretching
I heard the butterflies,
That everyone was catching
As I drifted down,
Earth so near
I knew that my parents
Soon would be here

Christine Almer,
Whitehouse Station

Inside And Outside Of The Window

Inside everyone wakes up like roosters on a farm.
Outside the children pretend they are buffalos on the plains.
Inside mom makes pancakes that are golden moons.
Outside yellow and black bees are doing the bumblebee jig.
Inside I paint pictures while colors dance through my head.
Outside children play basketball like professionals.
Inside my sister plays video games.
Outside the sun shines like a new CD
Inside my dad reads his lengthy book in his room.
Outside children on the sidewalk have lemonade stands.
Inside my brother watches movies in the family room.
Outside children ride bikes together on the street.

Jessica Cepparulo,
Scotch Plains

I'm The New Kid

Eighth graders ask me for money,
I'm the new kid.
Seventh graders ask me for fries,
I'm the new kid.
Sixth graders hate me,
I'm the new kid.
Fifth graders don't accept me,
I'm the new kid.
Fourth graders don't know me.
I'm the new kid.
What grade am I in?
You wouldn't know, cause
I'm the new kid.

Jeffrey McHale,
Bridgewater

Grandma Milana

Great memories with you
Relationships with you were the best
times of my life
And we always had a conversation
Nothing will keep your soul away
from me
Down here on earth is different than
heaven where you are now
My family misses you and are going
to really miss you on Mother's Day
And I know you're in a better place now,
but I can't help but to miss you too

Kerry Johnson,
Dunellen

Hero

When I think of a hero,
I think they are very strong,
but when I hear them coming,
I think there is nothing wrong.
Then I hear the thunder,
It gives me quite a scare,
Then I see the hero,
Knowing she will care.
I am very tired,
I want to get some rest,
My hero's there beside me,
I know she is the best.
Guess who is my hero,
My hero is my mother,
I give her a kiss goodnight
My mom is like no other.

Brooke Lathi,
Manville

Chapter 7
SIXTH GRADE

You Are My Hero

You are my hero
A light in the dark
In my heart, you leave a mark
You are my hero
Courageous and bold
Never afraid to do what you're told
You are my hero
So honest and true
What would America do without you
You are my hero
Never will I fear
Knowing that you always are here
You are my hero
No doubt in my mind
Because you, my hero, are one of a kind

Stephanie Grochowski,
Bridgewater

I Am An Orange

I am an orange.
I am orange.
I am a freshener for the Nilly's.
I live in a store with my whole family.
There are over a trillion oranges in my family.
It sounds exciting but it is not.
Because we get separated from each other.
Also ... sometimes I get eaten!
But, it is for my own good.
God is helping me get happy,
By when I get to heaven
I can wish for a good, healthy human body.
Humans are better.
But, I have to accept being an orange.
I have to accept the gift God gave me — a body and a life.
So, thank God for everything.

Shalini Chalikonda,
Raritan Borough

Untitled

You're walking down the street
When you trip in a hole
You think, "What rotten luck"
But keep walking to school

When you arrive at school
This big kid picks a fight
You think, "He's not so tough"
And you say alright

You limp into homeroom
With a black eye
Your teacher starts fussing
Like you just died

She sends you to the nurse
And there's a line
When you get to the front
She says you're just fine
Because of the line
It's gym, time block two
And by now,
No one wants to be you

Time block three
Yeah it was fine
No, it was great
But there's always the next line

Now it's language arts
Your weakest subject
Only one who got a C
You feel like a reject

5th period
Whizzed right by
You got in trouble

For making a girl cry

Finally
Lunch at last
But inside your lunchbox
A note said FAST

You walk to math
Calculator in pocket
Then you see that kid
Who put his fist in your socket

Onward to the nurse
You limp off again
The nurse says, "Now you're hurt,
Lay on the bed"

It's 8th period
Whew ISP
Now you're thinking
How do I survive as me?

School is finally over
You go on the bus
Sit next to some kids
All they do is cuss

When you get home
Your dog licks you for a while
You just look at him
And he makes you smile

Your mom then asks
Was school okay?
You look at your dog
"Yeah, a friend just made my day"

Dean Mauro,
Bridgewater

Dear Bad Dreams

Sometimes when I'm lying in my nice warm bed
you will pop into my head
You might not know who you are and what you do
but I'm here to remind you
You fill my head with scary thoughts, freaky visions
and then you leave me there in total shock
You make me pull my blankets up to my head and then leave me there looking
dead and in shock in my bed
You leave my teeth chattering, eyes looking back
and forth for imaginary ghost and goblins
lurking around my bed
I beg and I plead why can't you be happy dreams that put me right to sleep,
why can't you be filled with
ballerinas that dance around on their little tip toes
Why can't you be filled with houses made of candy
animals that are cute and birds that sing cute songs
and look really beautiful
But I guess no matter how much I beg and how much
I plead you just won't turn into happy dreams
But at least a girl can dream

Brielle Gomez,
Flemington

I Am

I am a quiet and caring girl who loves to cook.
I wonder how grandma makes such wonderful sweets that keep our mouths
watering for more.
I hear grandma talking with so much love and joy.
I see grandma as a sweet but wonderful loving woman.
I want to be a well-organized cook just like grandma.
I am a quiet and caring girl who loves to cook.
I pretend that I am a well-organized woman like grandma.
I feel my grandma's love which is very comforting to me.
I touch the clouds full and soft with grandma's love.
I worry that I will not receive grandma's gift of cooking.

I cry when grandma does not help me make my goodies to share with her.
I am a quiet and caring girl who loves to cook.
I understand my love for grandma is too strong to be broken.
I say that someday God should taste grandma's famous cookies filled with her love.
I dream that I will start my own goodie shop someday.
I try to keep up the good work and to never give up on my goals.
I hope that grandma's love will fill this world with the happiness she spreads.
I am a quiet and caring girl who loves to cook.

Suanne Traynor,
Flemington

The Lost Dragon

Above the golden rays of dawn, above the mighty sea,
A silver dragon in the clouds waiting faithfully.
Lost in his way, the path on which he sought.
Gone is the wind that made him tremble naught.
His wings that once caressed the air, now folded down without a care.
His eyes that once embraced the light are filled with wrath, filled with spite.
But calming is the melody that reached upon his ears.
A soft and sweet voice that many never hear.
His wings once more are spread out wide.
His soul once more is deep inside.
The wind blows past, forever to last.
The pathways to the skies are written in his eyes.
He swiftly soars away.

Katy Tkach,
Bridgewater

What Would You Do If You Won The Lottery

If you won the lottery, what would you do?
First I'd get a big house built that's defiantly brand new.
With shimmering lights, and golden chandeliers.
Then I'd buy a stereo so loud it'd definitely burst your ears!
Next I'd get a floor of trampolines
All the same color, Ninja Turtle green.
Then I'd get a bodyguard to keep away my sister that is very mean!
If you won the lottery, what would you do?
I'd buy a monkey and a bouncing kangaroo.
Well maybe not just the monkey or a kangaroo, maybe just a big zoo.
If you won the lottery, what would you do?
Well I would get Jason Kidd's autograph on my basketball shoe.
Next I'd buy an indoor pool with a springboard that blasts you high.
Then a concession stand that cooks a very crispy fry!
If you won the lottery, what would you do?
I'd buy some hot cars like a GTO, or a Mustang.
And maybe a paintball gun that goes bang!
If you won the lottery, what would you do?
I'd buy a bunch of land for a baseball park.
I'd get nice bats, gloves, and lights to play in the dark.
If you won the lottery, what would you do?
I'd get some quads and dirt bikes, too.
I'd most likely tear up the lawn, so I'd get a landscaper crew.
If you won the lottery, what would you do?

Robert George,
Bridgewater

I Am That

I could be the cool air
whipped around by the fan
or the warmth of the fire
by the hearth of your home.
I could be the envy in your
wicked sneer or the love

of another that draws you
close and near.
I could be a lot of things
But one thing is for sure.
I'll always be myself,
no matter how old I get
and how much I endure.

Tara Keane,
North Plainfield

Who Am I?

I am the rainbow that appears in the sky
I am the fragrance of a candle
I am the sun that sets on the ocean water
Next week, I will be a caterpillar
In two weeks, I will become a beautiful butterfly
I am the icing on a birthday cake
I am the ink in your pen
I am the paper that you write your feelings on
Next month, I will be a blooming flower
In five years, I will be graduating from high school
and going to college
Who am I?
I am Kiana Smiling

Kiana Smiling,
North Plainfield

Orange

Orange.
Orange is total and complete brightness.
Like a morning sunrise with light streaming through your window.
Orange is a light turned on to replace darkness,
Hundreds of bright colored flowers in a wide open field.
You can see them stretch for miles, looking never ending.
Orange is a bright sunny summer day.
Orange is the feeling you have on the last day of school counting seconds until the bell,
And the feeling you have when doing something you love.
Now you can feel Orange.

Joey Usifer,
Belle Mead

My Sister Is A Bug

A funny poem inspired by Jack Prelusky

My sister is a bug,
She is smaller than my shoe.
She eats green leaves and
Is filled with gushy goo.
My sister is a bug,
She doesn't like fly swatters
My parents can't believe
An insect is their daughter.
My sister is a bug;
she lives in animal fur,
She made lots of noise
Until I stepped on her.

Nadine Skowronek,
Bridgewater

This Is Where You'll Find Me

Sitting in a chair at a computer
Instant messaging my friends
Talking about anonymous things
Keeping friendship in.
One of my friends ask,
"Want to play checkers."
"Sure. Checkers it is."
Moving pieces and getting kings,
As I try to win.
I happily play,
Treasuring the gift of friendship.

Aarifah Bacchus,
Somerville

Acceptance

She's too short
He's too tall
Her eyebrows are too thick
And his nose is too small
She paints her nails black
He always wears a tie
She'll never smile
He'll never cry
No one should be judged
No one should hurt from something you say
No one should be excluded
And most of all, no one should be treated
this way.

Siara Sealy,
North Plainfield

Sanctuary

I know the language of my room
where I sleep, read and do my homework
Its walls provide a sanctuary for me
a place I can peacefully stay,
My fan talks with his arms and clicking sound
at night and I listen to it,
My windows show interest with big open eyes
As the blinds whisper with a whooshing sound
Every time I pull on the string to open or close it,
My bed, my blanket and pillow work together
To keep me snug, safe, and warm at night,
My books on a shelf are patiently waiting to be read,
The trash can gobble up and treasure,
The things I don't need
and cries when it's emptied
So I fill it back up again,
The pencils in my pencil case fear I'll break
Their freshly sharpened tips,
The legs of the desk sink into the soft dusk colored rug
That cushions my feet,
The couch softens
every time I sit down to read,
I know the language of my room.

Elizabeth Tubito,
Flemington

A Day at School

Math is dull
History's boring
Gym is exhausting
I'd rather be snoring.
Lunch goes too fast
Homeroom's too slow
Skills is a drag
I'm dying to go.
It's finally here
The end of day bell
I am so happy
I just want to yell!
But then I realized
While screaming hooray,
School's kind of cool
I'll miss it someday.

Christina Jedra,
North Plainfield

Untitled

If war was peace ...
If hate was love ...
If stealing was giving ...
If violence was kindness ...
If bullying was comforting ...
If hitting was hugging ...
If weapons were flowers ...
If killing was loving ...
If evil was good ...
If death was life ...
The world would be a better place.

Danielle MacMath,
Bridgewater

Ode To The Dogs

Ode to the dogs, chasing a ball
With tongues lolling out
On a hot summers day
Ode to the dogs, playing and running
Never ending chasing
Who knows what they're thinking
Ode to the water, that rejuvenates dogs
Filling them with life and energy
A never ending power source
Ode to the puppies
With their sad little eyes
That melt your heart with compassion
Ode to the hunting dog
Tall and gallant
Risking life and limb for master
Ode to the house dog
Warm in the winter
Refreshing in the summer
And always there to comfort you
Ode to all dogs
Large and small
Beautiful or homely
Man's best friend

Thomas Fellin,
Somerville

Untitled

Daringly I climb trees.
A flyin' through the air, off branches.
Never quit trying until I could climb the tree.
After a while, I climbed like a monkey.
Finish climbing and leave it behind - never!
I can climb three trees very high.
No! I don't want to come in for dinner.
Eat? I'll eat in the tree.

Mmm, eating in a tree - yum, yum, yum.
After I'm finished, maybe a nap?
No, too early, still time to play.

Dana Fineman,
Flemington

I Am

I am a lighthearted girl who adores horses.
I wonder if there is a horse out there just waiting for me.
I hear their whinnies echoing all around me.
I see them racing the wind, free and reckless.
I want to fly like an eagle, to where I belong.
I am a lighthearted girl who adores horses.

I pretend to be a horse whisperer.
I feel the power of their free hearts.
I touch their velvety, gleaming coats.
I worry that their faith in people will be broken.
I cry when a horse is mistreated.
I am a lighthearted girl who adores horses.

I understand when a horse longs to be free once more.
I say, Let your heart run free.
I dream of when I will work with horses every day.
I try to make others see horses the way I do.
I hope that I will be able to soothe the wounds I find in horses.
I am a lighthearted girl who adores horses.

Donna Andres,
Basking Ridge

Parts Of My Heart

I've given part of my heart away
To family and friends alike
Parts of my heart have been torn away
Parts of my heart are gone
A friend, I thought cheerful and loyal
One day deserted me
A man, the closest thing I've had to a grandfather
Passed away one day
My best bud, packs up and prepares to move
Move to somewhere, it seems, a million miles away
And as these people come and go
So do pieces of my heart
A portion of me is missing
A portion of me is gone

Erin Stoyell-Mulholland,
High Bridge

Memories

What are memories, some would say pictures, or even trophies.
What are memories, what would you say. I would say it's something you
would remember, so are pictures, trophies, home movies, or even a letter.
But do you know what it really is?
What are memories, it's not trophies cause when trophies turn to rust and
pictures full of dust or even when movie tapes break, you have your
memory, that's what memories are. Your memory is all it takes.

Chelsea Deonarine,
Somerset

Chapter 8
SEVENTH GRADE

Beautiful, Caring, Loving ... Gone

Sounds of chirping birds
Mourning a loss
A call
Earlier that day
Told my mom her niece passed away
She spilled the news to me
I cried hysterically
Beautiful, caring, loving ...
Gone
Two kids left with their non-caring dad, too
My mom was so mad, so blue
Why did this have to happen? Why me?
Death, after death in our family
Beautiful, caring, loving ...
Gone
No comfort
Miles away in Europe
We traveled after
A mess
They lived their lives around her, now dead
In her coffin, beautiful and still
So far away from love
Beautiful, caring, loving ...
Gone
I love her
So far away
Still in my heart
Beautiful, caring, loving ...
Here

Anna Tichy,
Martinsville

This Cage

I've lived here
my entire life,
and still no one
knows who I am.
I live in this cage,
and will never
come out
I'm invisible
to the human eye,
when people pass me by,
I have nothing to say.
Neither do they,
because I live in a cage,
that no one can see.
When ever I speak
the words never come,
And if they do
they'll never be
what I wanted to say.
Because this cage blocks
my voice anyway.
I feel like that something
surrounds me,
Everyday of my life,
A cage with a lock
that I won't be able
to take off.
And it will always
take my voice and
feelings away,
But when the day comes,
I'll come out.
And tell,
what I've wanted to say,
this whole entire time.

Sarah Greenstone,
Bridgewater

Keep Searching

When everything is quiet
There is...
Peacefulness
Alone here with your troubles
Alone in this immense world
Where nothing matters
Peacefulness washes you away
When everything is quiet
There is...
Loneliness
Everything around you has stopped
One step away from you
Alone in this world with no one to trust
Running as fast as you can
Time just limping after you
No use
Loneliness just sweeps you away
When everything is quiet
There is...
The tall tree dwarfing you
standing so small next to it
Feeling out of place
feeling not you
When everything is quiet ...
you find yourself
searching deep within
digging your heart out
like it was a treasure hunt
You hold it close
not letting go
For you have found
the most important thing for you ...
the purpose of life
NEVER let it go.

Stephanie Huang,
Bound Brook

Girls And Boys

Girls are said to be smart.
Boys don't know at all what life is.
Girls are sacred, to be kept well.
Boys — laugh too much.
Girls study, lots and lots
Boys don't — study at all.
Girls like flowers,
Boys like bees
The flower rises beautifully
and that's all the bee sees.
Girls are beautiful inside out.
Boys only care — about the outside.

*Luisa Grisales,
North Plainfield*

Abbey

My owner loves it when I steal her brand new leather shoe
Which then I take to the corner and I begin to chew
My owner loves it when I shred the plastic on the ground
And she has to pick up all the pieces that are lying all around
My owner loves it when every minute she has to let me out
So I can go outside and smell all the things about
My owner loves it when I bark and never quit,
And when she tries to stop me and she can't, she throws a fit
But my owner once told me, even though I fool around
That I will always be her little beagle hound

*Jessi Brygier,
Bridgewater*

A Blood-Red Morn

On the march
Through thickets
Of untracked terrain
In enemy territory
Germany, 1942

The whole world
Is a sudden-death battle
Every shot
Like a storm
Causing damage and death
In large battles
Troops from both sides
Fight to the death
With guns in their arms
And hatred in their hearts
The bullets shred
Through anything
And everything
Claiming lives and souls
Bodies lie
Around
Unclaimed
Then buried
In forgotten mass graves
And as dawn does break
And the sky looks down
Far it is known
Blood hath been shed this night
And many will not return home
Germany, 1942

C. M. Gabbett,
Raritan Borough

Only You

Only you can hold me in your arms the way you do.
You are the one I can trust with all my secrets.
You stay close to me in heart to heart
face to face, true love to true love,
Only you can love me the way you do.
Only you belong with me now and forever.
It is you the only one for me and for you.
Only you forever.

Anthony Kowal,
Bridgewater

But I'm Never Alone

I seem to walk with every beady eye watching me
I seem to walk with every face
shooting bombs of laughter at me
I seem to walk with no one at my side to feel the hurt within me
I seem to walk with Loser and Freak pinned on my soul
They buzz inside, stinging me with hurt
But I'm never alone
Someone's out there feeling my pain
She's like the brightest star
Like an angel there to keep me going
The words may hurt
The words may kill
But I'm never alone
She's always there
To bear my life
When it topples over me
To be chased with me
Sad with me
To feel sorrow tingle down my back
To keep me from dying
From suffering
From drowning at the bottom of
loneliness
And being alone in the corner
So ...
I seem to walk now
Waiting for her smile
When nothing else is right
And I seem to walk now
Waiting for myself to shine
In this dark world
Because I'm never alone

Gloria Chen,
Bridgewater

I Hate My Chores

After dinner every evening at exactly six-thirty
I see the pile of dishes sitting there, dirty
I hate my chores
All the leftover food is engraved in the dishes
Like how my clothes are "stuck" on the floor
I have to scrub and scrub and scrub and scrub
Just my luck
I hate my chores
I must wash the dishes quick
So I don't miss my television shows
And usually I drop a dish
And it shatters before my toes
Crash!
I hate my chores
As soon as my mom hears the ear-splitting sound
She comes running into the kitchen
With a face as red as a nose on a clown
I hate my chores
She tries to contain her anger
But I can still picture smoke coming out of her ears
I apologize and race to my room
Knowing I'll be grounded for the next 10 years
I hate my chores
As if doing the dishes wasn't enough
I have other chores that aren't as tough
I must clean my room and make by bed
And feed my dog, the quadruped
I hate my chores
Now, having run out of things to say
I guess I will go do my chores
Good day!

Monica Patel,
Bridgewater

Dreams

I dream of you and me together
I dream of us holding hands forever
I can feel your kiss on my lips
I can feel your hands on my hips
I can feel your love in the air
I can feel everything around me so fair
But now I know they're only dreams
But I wish they were as real as they seemed
As the years slowly pass by
I notice something as I looked at the sky
I notice that I have no love left for you
But I'm not sure if it could be true
I seem to have forgotten you in my mind
A thought in the past that was left behind
A love that will never be found
A love that was never bound

Celine Sunga,
Piscataway

Nature Is Old

Nature is old
She turned old long ago
But when she was young
She was deprived
Jump-by-jump
Everyone took from her
Outside beauty
Until only one
Her thought
That beauty was in
Her giving
Not herself
Striking beauty
Jerked you
Between the eyes

Long ago
Were you jerked
Did you ever help?
Through her brilliant, floundering jerk
In between her eyes
Her winter pine
In death
Shines
Shines tin tingly
Have you ever
Seen it
Shine?
Shine tin tingly
No
Of course not!
You would rather bring flakey
Destruction upon her shine
Go ahead
Her thought of beauty was in
Her dazzling years
As dazzling
As a fiery star
And her giving to the fossilized
She is old
She turned old
Long ago

Lauren Hendricks,
Bound Brook

The Night Sky

In the night sky
Blackness spreads through the earth
As the night is giving birth
To all the objects twirling 'round
The sky so sweet and sound
And if the brightness is not seen
The night sky will no longer be
But tonight, tonight
The sky shines
In the night sky
The moon
So soon
Comes up
And up
In the sky
The sun dies
A smile curves up
To fill a brand new cup
Of shine and sparkle
Looking divine
Spread throughout the
universe
In the night sky
The stars
Vibrant as Mars
Dance in the air
Without a care, circling
They are guides
Deciding
The sky
Which will shoot or pass by
Like the clouds with the sun
Like one they blend
Spread throughout the
universe
In the night sky
The leaves

Fall from the trees
They dance and prance
To the song of the cricket
All night long
A sweet lullaby
Up and,
Up
Spread throughout the
universe
The night sky
Soon will die
When the sun peeks through
The dew of morning
The moon waves goodbye
and rises high
With the stars
Like vibrant Mars
And leaves
That from the trees do fall
They wave goodbye
Into the night sky

Julia Murray,
Bridgewater

Untitled

I love to have fun on a warm summer day
When you can look outside and watch little kids play
Memories of summer when I was just small
I keep them forever as long as I can recall
Sitting and sipping lemonade under a tree
Even the bad ones like getting stung by a bee
But the moment I see the first flowers bloom
I know that summer will be coming soon

Amy Evanylo,
Manville

When I Was A Clutz

When I was little, I was a Clutz
Bam, Crash, Boom
I was like the shattered cup on the floor
I quickly swept it up with a broom
When I was little, I was a Clutz
Splat, Splash, Smack
I dropped a can of soda
I wiped it up before my mom came back
When I was little, I was a Clutz
Wham, Crack, Thump
I tipped over my mother's vase
It hit my foot and gave me a lump
When I was little, I was a Clutz
Tear, Cut, Snip
Oops, I cut my sister's history project
Do you think she'll notice the rip?
When I was little, I was a Clutz
Tick, Tock, Tick
I bumped my head against the wall
That's why my nickname's slick

Mike Crooks,
Bridgewater

Summer Woodlands

Cotton-candy clouds
Drop their load of bombs
Water droplets and all of the
Woodland creatures retreat to their homes
Like they were running for their lives.
When the rain stops,
The throat clogging dampness
Of the wilderness green
Clogs your throat
The soft rumble of thunder fills the air
And fades as

It gets further and further away,
And the sun slowly rises
Like a clock ticking
The hours of the day away

Ryan Prochko,
Martinsville

My Brothers

Stephen
He's the oldest
He's the tallest
He's everything I'm not
He sleeps a lot — Slumber!
He complains a lot — Boohoo!
And he's everything I'm not

Scott
He's the coolest
He's the bravest
He's everything I'm not
He leaves — Freedom!
He screams — Screech!
And he's everything I'm not

Shaun
He says he's the coolest
He says he's the bravest
He says he's everything I'm not
He says he's good — Honorable!
He says he's the best — Prime!
And I say ...
He's right!
He's everything I'm not.

Stewart Woodruff,
Bridgewater

Darkest Before Dawn

There's rock-hard ground beneath me
Iron-metal chains on my wrists
Cold-hearted darkness surrounds me,
Anger lives in my fists.
The frozen-black, it holds me
My spirit, almost gone
But then my hope shall keep me —
It's always darkest before dawn.
Danger lurks behind me,
On little cat-footed feet
Bad things like to scare me
When we least expect to meet.
I feel warm ground beneath me
I spy a ray of light
Pools of heat are on me —
The sun will make things right.
Danger flees from me
So frightened by the light
Bad luck screams behind me
Searching for the night
As inner-strength threads through me
The darkness truly gone
I know this light shall save me —
It's always darkest before dawn.

Beatrice Cayaban,
Bound Brook

Into The Night

Into the night, the dark night, the dark moonlit night
The sun has gone away, and the town is hushed by
A blanket of darkness
And all the night creatures come out to play
Into the night, the dark night, the dark moonlit night

The bats dance through the sky like
A waterfall rushing
The foxes crawl through the grass
Sneaking up on small rodents and
Playing hide-n-go eat
And the cats on the wooden fence
Paw each other 'till
They lose their balance, then fall to the ground, and land
Silently on their feet
Into the night, the dark night, the dark moonlit night
A mouse and his brother snatch
Cheddar cheese from the traps set up
While they squeak in laughter
The squirrels in the attic fight
Nuts into secret corners and
Skitter daintily back to their tree homes
And the birds try to get inside windows to make nests
By hammering their beaks against the panes of glass
And then they eventually
Give up
And settle in a tree
Into the morning, the 8 a.m. morning, the 8 a.m. orange jewel morning
The town pushes off its
Blanket of darkness
And is yawning awake to
A bright cloudless sky
And the day creatures
Sit down for breakfast
Talking and sharing new dreams
And all this time the night creatures are spying and waiting,
for when they can go
Into the night, the dark night, the dark moonlit night
Again

Rachael Clinton,
Bridgewater

What It's Like To Be Me

crazy Go
nothing there's until Try
expectations High
something worth it's know you, But
life my in day A
lazy be Can't
Stressing
Working
Perfecting
life my in day A
sound every With
feeling every With
moment Every
appearing is truth The
life my in day A
around goes world The
now backwards Or
confusing, confused, confused, confusing, confused, Confused
?how know, and know I Will
life my in day A
empty goes mind My
event big every At
lost seems answer The
scent no, behind Left
life my in day A
?me lend to should a have anyone Does
fall to about I'm
backs stabbing, hearts breaking, lines Crossing
?all you won't, up me help You'll
life my in day A
think you Now
bad too isn't It
blink a in gone to could troubles Your
glad are you and, smile just you If
sad are you when Remember
life tasted ain't You
Until

lived You've
life my in day A

Somya Sharma,
Martinsville

Sea Of Solitude

I weep into the depths of a solemn emptiness
No one to share my secrets
The echoes whisper silently
As I drift in a haze of solitude

Shadows are my only friends
They flicker 'round my eyes
The light is like a stream of hope
In an empty world of dusk and dark

The silence is a pillow
Smothering my dreams
Of reaching the surface again
And returning to the joy

In a jubilant thrust
I brush through the veil
Between light and dark
Happiness fills my soul
And floods my heart

I breathe freely
And feel the sounds of life
The loneliness has lost its grip
And drowned in a pool of hope

Emily Susko,
Bridgewater

A Walk Through Everything

Today I am going on a walk
Many wonderful things, I shall see
When I walk along the riverbank
I see a school of fish, shining bright, jumping up to greet me
I see rowboat moored to an old pier, swaying in the wind
When I walk over an old rustic bridge
I see the clear aqua sparkling water below me
I see a man walking the other way and say "Good morning."
When I walk into the little town
I see children playing, effervescent as ever
I see a busy lane with people going to shops, work places, houses
When I walk down a farm road leading out of town
I see farms all around, yellow fields as far as the eye could see
I see an ancient rattletrap bus carrying country people into town
When I walk up to a farmhouse
I see a kind lady who treats me to a delicious meal
I see cows grazing on the green, rolling pasture
When I walk into the woods at the edge of the farm
I see brown trees, bright trees, alive trees, dead trees
I see an adroit red fox, prowling, looking, its eyes missing nothing
When I walk down the trail, my feet crunch-crunching on the leaves
I see a clearing, a very small one indeed
In that clearing, a small wooden cabin in which an old man lives
When I walk to the door of the intrepid, lonely man
He offers his wrinkled hand after opening the creaky old door
I take it; I shake it and say, "How do you do?"
He then replies, "I'm fine, how are you?"
He beckons me in, asks me to stay the night
We sit up late by the firelight, telling many tales
I wake up at the crack of dawn
Today I am going on a walk
Many wonderful things, I shall see.

Vivek Prakash,
Bridgewater

Seashore

Time goes by slow
And a hurt pangs through my heart
You got to go with the flow
Even though we're apart

You'll never know how I miss you
When no one's there to hold my hand
My whole life has gone askew
And nothing's gone as we'd planned

Although Hope may seem hollow
When life seems without cause
And there's no one to follow
Nothing is as it was

Growing up can be hard
Leaving childhood behind
You can't let down your guard
Nothing's harsher than mankind

So when I'm sad and alone
And it seems no one is there
I step out of the unknown
And I remember where

When my mother was holding me
Rocking my head in her hands
As we looked out at the sea
Only a mother understands

Veronica Ward,
Bridgewater

The Leaf

I walked down a cool, mid-autumn path,
With no set destination,
When with no warning, from above,
Came a single leaf.

I took the leaf into my hand,
A very lifeless brown,
With curvatures so boldly lines
Throughout its dying body.

So I gazed up towards the heavens,
And saw a giant oak,
Deciduous by nature's law,
Thus it was now leafless.

Once it had been great and green,
Flourishing with joy,
But, alas, spring came and went,
Winter began his conquest.

I looked down at the leaf I held,
This barren tree's last treasure,
Taken away by nature's force,
Too strong to even resist.

Though this is the place and time,
When the tree is mourning,
I took some comfort in my knowing,
It will be green again.

I dropped the leaf and walked away,
I'm lifeless brown for now,
Nature took my grandpa from me,
But I'll be green again.

Kirk Geritano,
Edison

The Not So Boring Class

One spring-like day in April
my English class took a nature walk on a dark, long beaten path.
We were solemn through the graveyard; yet
happy outside the fence of stillness.
The flowers of all different sorts,
seemed to be welcoming us, by wavering in the breeze.
On that day, we were taught the names of flowers,
instead of boring prepositions.
The walk, oh! What more there is to say,
the colors and vibrance of each is so special in itself.
The colors made the graveyard come alive,
in a way of friendliness.
The class that day was fun,
filled with joy, happiness, and laughter.
In my long life I hope to live,
I anticipate another class like this one.

Lucila Sparkes,
Hillsborough

Untitled

I am ... gentle
I am ... tough
I am ... darkness
I am ... beautiful
I am ... my sins
I am ... a flower
I am ... a brick wall
I am ... the blowing wind
I am ... as gentle as the blowing wind
I am ... carrying the darkness of my sins
I am ... as beautiful as a flower
I am ... as tough as a brick wall
Really I am ... a confused soul

Kayla Young,
Piscataway

Hunting

Stalking through the jungle night
The tiger chased and tried to bite
The wart hog sensed danger and ran
in fright.
Until he had enough courage to turn
and fight.

I climbed up a tree
So they wouldn't see me.
I thought it was wrong
But the battle was long.

The tiger got his meat
Now the story is done.
So let's go home
And have some fun.

Kyle Koemm,
Somerville

Her Stories

Her stories
My ears
Solid listening —
Heart beat beat
Her heart has so ... many
Stories I want to hear
Stories that make me want to live forever
All the questions I have
Ones that got answered
Ones that never will get answered
Ones that are still in my head
Much time has been wasted
Sitting on her couch
Sitting quietly

Sitting patiently as her stories evolve
Her stories
My ears
Solid listening —
Heart beat beat

Alyson Furda,
Martinsville

LIFE Poem

Life is a gamble
It's random at any rate
You may be dealt four aces
Or a few deuces
Hope for a straight

Life presents a cornucopia of choices
Take a chance
Play the odds
Give life a nod
Find your gold romance

Life is worth living
With its ups and downs
At times frustrating and disappointing
But also challenging and rewarding and exciting and invigorating
Enjoy each day's sun-ups and sun-downs

Life is an eggshell walk
Through which you amble
Master not of your fate
Random as a first blind date
Life is a gamble

Nick McGahan,
Bridgewater

INK
by Gray

Pen and paper
Inkwell and ink
Soft in my hand
Telling what I think
Colors in my mind
Blue, green, yellow, red
When they come together
In their true form
I shall write my poems
This is the norm
I weave them all together
Like a woman at her loom
Some are bright and lively
Others dark and silent like a tomb
They all go together
Fitting inside my head, or
Sitting on this paper
Waiting to be read
Secrets whispers what I think
Everything wrote down in ink

Chelsea Reimer,
Bound Brook

I Am

I am many words
I am a reflection
I am thoughts
I am memories
I am a billboard
I am a mirror
I am a letter

I am a picture
I am the many words on a billboard
I am a clean cute reflection in a mirror
I am the best thoughts in a letter
I am the greatest memories in a picture
I am an alternate person in this reality called life.

LeeAnn Ielmini,
Piscataway

Why?

Why do you hate me?
Why can't you see?
Why I love you so much?
Why can't we be in touch?
Why can't our love rise?
Why does it always die?
Why can't it be true?
Why can't it be what I want to do?
Why does it have to be this day?
Why can it be by our favorite bay?
Why don't you want my heart?
Why can't you just be smart?
Why can't you call me honey?
Why can't you be sunny?
Why can't you be here?
Why can't you be near?
Why can't I have the power?
Why are you like a dumb flower?
Why do you hate me?
Why can you see?

Candi Fritzinger,
South Bound Brook

The Duck That Couldn't Quack

Yes, I'm a duck, an odd one too
Here's my story, you may not have knew
I'm unique, not like others
Different than my brothers
'Cause quacking is what I cannot do

Quack, Quack

Some people can't hear, some people can't see
I was born without quacking, that's just me
There are days when I'm mad
But most days I'm so glad
That I'm my marvelous me, Heehee!

Quack, Quack

Some ducks make fun of the way I go
I find it cruel, just to let you know
I don't see how they're so mean
I'm not happy, not so keen
Sometimes, I want to shout, Oh No!

Quack, Quack

The others don't realize we're all the same
After all, we're all ducks, who am I to blame?
They also don't see
That quacking to me
Is just as strange as thinking NOT quacking is lame!

Quack, Quack

Zach Sitrin,
Bridgewater

Dance

She dreams of being on the stage
Her name upon the program page
Days, months and years she's trained
Poise and confidence she gained
Pink ribbons tied and staying
Laced from an old Pointe shoe
Satin, worn and fraying
They've seen a dance or two
Once again she points her toe
Upon the floor of dance
She leaps, she spins, she turns today
Just waiting for her chance

Jordan Kaschak,
Bridgewater

I Am

I am a pleasant memory.
I am laughter.
I am sounds.
I am thoughts.
I am a picture album.
I am a joke book.
I am speakers used to play jazz music.
I am a journal of an adventurer.
I am a pleasant picture in an album of memories.
I am the laughter after reading a humorous joke book.
I am the sound of jazz coming from speakers.
I am the thoughts recorded in a journal as someone has an adventure.
Really I am just a shy, 12-year-old boy writing a poem for a class.

Alvin Yanza,
Piscataway

Dear Math Homework,

I have you almost every day,
You're always there when I want to play.
Looming over me like a bad dream,
Always more challenging than you seem.
How about you do yourself for a change!
You figure out the median, mode and range!
I just want to get up and run,
To play outside all day in the sun ...
But you keep me inside,
So in the house I reside.
I could finally get you done,
But figuring you out isn't very fun.
Too many numbers and problems to do,
I need to know fractions, and negatives too!
Oh why can't you just disappear,
Can't you see I DON'T WANT YOU HERE!

Samantha Towle,
Three Bridges

Thinking About Summer

I'm thinking of having no homework to do
I'm thinking of buying something brand new
I'm thinking of sleeping all I want
And always eating at my favorite restaurant

I'm thinking of school being over real soon
I'm thinking about looking at the full moon
I'm thinking about my hair not being curly
and not having a single care or worry

Though thinking about these things is quite a bummer
When I'm stuck shoveling snow thinking about summer

Alisha McClain,
Piscataway

Summer

It's melted-ice-cream hot
In the summer
Splashing kids are jumping, bumping in the water
School kids sleeping late
Kids and parents are at the beach
Yelling and screaming, bury me in the sea sand
As the whispering breeze sneeze comes ashore
Like a refreshing glass of lemonade
It's melted-ice-cream hot
In the summer
It's melted-ice-cream hot
In the summer
Air conditioners on high
While bills are sky high
Kids are screaming, dreaming, playing, staying
It's melted-ice-cream hot
In the summer

Crystal Condit,
Watchung

Amazing Creature

Look at the amazing creature soar over the sunset
See its amazing features — bluish with an orange sun tint
What can this astounding being be?
Look at its astounding leaps; Leaping wave by wave
It jumps way up high into the fresh, sea air, smiling blissfully...
What is this astonishing creature?
See its warm, loving heart caring for all the things in the ocean
It has a mind of a million minds, an I.Q. of a thousand, like an aquatic Einstein
This creature has so many fantastic traits
I don't know of many creatures such as this
But there is only one animal living on this earth with such amazement...
A dolphin!

Leandra Del Pozo,
Bridgewater

Insomniac

Ribbons of rainbow light play inside closed eyelids
Trying to create dreams and summon sleep
The hearing has become so acute as to hear a pin drop
Any excuse to sit up
Start tossing and turning, there's no way to get comfortable under the fluffy comforter
Guilt is now gnawing at the stomach, remembering tomorrow's commitments
Won't muster up the courage to cast a sidelong glance at the sharply glowing neon
numbers on the clock, penetrating the darkness.
See how little time there is left before dawn breaks
Unfortunately, right when you feel yourself start to slip away into darkness...
Then, the harsh piercing cry of the alarm clock slashing across the dark peace of the primitive morning.
Another sleepless night to add to the overgrown collection.

Chelsea Ihling,
Neshanic Station

Three-Toned Poem

Some days I'm a sunrise pink
ready to wake up the world with my energy
and make someone's day brighter
Other days I'm a midnight blue.
Sleepy, grouchy and tired
ready to make someone's day miserable
Some days I'm a sea green
peaceful, friendly, and relaxed
and think with my head

Ariana Jimenez,
Piscataway

Sixth Grade

It all began in sixth grade,
when I started to feel betrayed.
My friends didn't really talk to me
and there was no "we."
Then I met new friends
and we'll be friends to the end.
We were best friends in an instant.
We stay together no matter the distance.
Together we went to the movies and the mall,
winter, spring, summer, and fall.
I'll always remember sixth grade was strange
because it was the year everything changed.

Jackie Souksay,
Piscataway

My Terribly-Good Family

I am thankful for my terribly-good family
I am thankful for my can't-be-quiet sister
I am thankful for my go-get-your-math-book mother
I am thankful for my just-eat-the-thing grandmother
I am thankful for my can't-help-today father
I am thankful for my what-are-you-trying-to-do-raise-my-bills grandfather
I'm thankful for my not-when-I-can-play-my-video-games cousin
I'm thankful for my wash-my-muddy-paws dog
I'm thankful for my I'm-telling-on-you cousin
I am thankful for my terribly-good family

Nolan Cirillo-Penn,
Bridgewater

Hope

Hope is a pretty, pink, petal-filled flower
She stands gracefully
Gently moving side to side from the soft pushing of the wind
She gets harder and harder
And colder and colder
The pretty, pink, petal-filled flower is now shattered, helpless
Dead
Leaves are shattered helpless
Dead
Houses are frosted with snow and dangling icicles
It's dark
Too dark
A sudden streak of light breaks through the sky
It gets brighter and brighter
Colors such as green and
yellow appear
A bud
A precious bud
A pretty, pink bud has matured and becomes
Hope
Hope is a pretty, pink, petal-filled flower
She stands tall
Tall and proud

Anisha Pandya,
Bridgewater

He Used To Be

He used to love me,
He used to talk to me,
He used to play with me,
He used to be all I ever had,
He used to be a good person,
He used to be my best friend,
He used to live with my family,
He used to help me through every day,

He used to be someone I looked up to,
He used to be the brightest part of my day,
He used to be the only humor I ever received,
He used to be a special part of my life,
He used to be my brother!

Zoya Shamsi,
Piscataway

LIFE

Life is an endless portal.
Going and going and going.
This life portal never ends.
Until you black out.
Then...
No more hope.
No more light.
No more portals.
No more life.
Life is an endless portal.
Until you die.
That is when the portal closes.
No more chances.
You exceeded your limit.
Your life ended.
Just like the portal.
THAT'S IT.
YOU'RE DONE

Jared Simon,
Bridgewater

Cleaning My Room

Although it's so easy to dirty a room
It's not so easy to clean
I can throw stuff everywhere...
And really not seem to care
There's blue jeans
And jelly beans
Also some wrinkled shirts
And black shirts
The point is it's just so messy!
With chips and candy
And piles of books
Which might even touch the hook...
On my ceiling!
I try and try and just give up
But then my mom screams, look up!
There it is standing so high
My pile of clothes touching the sky
Clean your room she shouts!
Do I dare pull one out?
There's old chewing gum stuck to my floor
And piles of old papers blocking the door
I sigh and sigh and huff and puff
Till I finally picked my room up
My mom remembers what I did
And I'm proud of my clean room
The hour was getting much too late
But I'm happy that I met my fate!

Lucy Roseo,
South Plainfield

Useless Things

A pen without ink
A kitchen without a sink
A friend without care
A game that's not fair

A house without a door
An apple without a core
A store without money
A clown that's not funny

A person without a name
An actor without his fame
A cake without frosting
A cross without crossing

A country without a flag
A commercial without a snag
A year without days
A dreamer without gaze

*Sarah Beleski,
Piscataway*

He Was Lost At Sea

He is lost at sea
What would you do?
The blue, peaceful water and cloudless sky are like an endless summer day
He is sad because he might not see his family again
"What shall I do?" He says out loud but no one hears him,
The hot pacific sun hangs in the still sky
He waits patiently ... for someone to rescue him

*Ben Klitenick,
Bridgewater*

Will

Will I go on to win?
I am close to my goal.
Laughing at my past obstacles.
Last one's the hardest though.

*Andrew Specian,
Bound Brook*

I'm From

I'm from a middle-class family,
with many qualities.
I'm from St. Peter's Hospital,
I'm from God and His clay,
I'm from a cul-de-sac,
I'm from New Jersey,
I'm from America,
I'm from Hidden Trail,
I'm from my ancestry,
I'm from Lanston,
to Martin Luther King
to Rosa Parks.
This is where I'm from.

Jerome Coney III,
North Plainfield

Eruption Of Life

My life is like a volcano.
I have built it on eruptions of anger and sadness,
And the happiness that grows out of
the fertile ash of pain that follows.

Each eruption tears down my walls of self-confidence,
Leaving me vulnerable, and discouraged.
Those walls keep everything out.
Without them there is a bombardment of
Sounds, feelings and an
Overwhelming sense that someone's watching you.

My painful memories are stored up tight,
Deep within the crater of my mind
But in those eruptions, they overflow,
Taking over my thoughts and actions,
Overwhelming my better memories,
Those growing like great trees out of the flowers of my happiness,

Those memories that define who I am.
At times, the eruptions seem like a faraway dream,
But when they do happen, it's not me,
I just spit out whatever comes to mind,
Not hiding the painful truths away,
With the memories in the crater.
And then, it's over. I cry. Like rain on hot lava,
It cools me down, sealing up the crater with the memories that can kill.
But during those times, I really need those walls,
Because even the slightest disruption
Can bring the lava back up, destroying all the
repairs I worked for,
And there are a lot of disruptions after an eruption.

Yet, as each eruption brings more hate, pain and sadness,
It builds me higher, makes me stronger, and
It prepares me for life to come.

Athena Ierokomos,
Flemington

Life

My tears burn like the endless
Fire of the place I dare not speak
With so much pain and sorrow that wanders inside me
And yet I remain here still and silent
Afraid what is around the next corner
And I wish with all my might someday
Somehow that all this pain and suffering
Would just go
But the evil consumes and the helpless are forgotten because they seem to not
matter and with money how could that help
For the eternal God tries to help but the power of evil is just too strong
And
If life were cherished
Then maybe the burning
Tears just might stop.

Lisa Avery,
Whitehouse Station

I Didn't Do My Homework

Knock
Knock
Knock
Uh-oh, my mom's home
And
I didn't do my homework
I didn't study for the test
I didn't do my reading —
Instead I took a rest

I studied for five minutes
My head just couldn't think —
Instead I took a tasty snack
And drunk right from the sink

I didn't read
I didn't study
I didn't do my homework —
But that's Okay
Because today there wasn't homework anyway
I didn't do my homework!

Chris Banafato,
Bridgewater

Spring Flow

The wind a living jewel
So very very cool
The leaves are starting to jump up high
The small streams match the blue sky
Little cotton tails in their holes
While on the grass puppies roll
The geese flying north pull in spring
Flap! Flap! Honk! Wing by wing

John Wilkinson,
Bridgewater

My Crazy Little Town

Wild neighborhood
Crazy neighborhood trouble
Loud kids
Broken window — crash
Crowded street
They have had enough people
Annoyed cops
Sprinting kids
Best friend — BJ
Outside cats
Barking dogs
Passed football
Wounded cars
Wild neighborhood

Bruno Riga,
Bridgewater

Mountains

Smooth and silent
Bright and quiet
Always delightful, mountains
To reach the top
To see the hawks
Such a heavenly view it is
To fly so high —
So high in the sky
So you feel like a light-winged bird
Oh, but the mountains
The rolling mountains
Is everything the Earth could ever be

Matthew Riley,
Martinsville

Picture Perfect

Take a deep breath and close your eyes,
Block out the pain, the tears and the lies.
Picture the world like a painting so bright,
The colors so vibrant, the feelings so right.
Look at the people, their smiles so broad.
They're so truthfully happy, you can't see a fraud.
They don't need to hide stories, more heartbreaking
than the last.
You don't see them in wheelchairs, in hospitals or casts.
Now take out the smiles till there are only tears.
Darken the sky above a world made of fears.
Replace your deep breath with a gasp or a fuss.
That looks familiar, oh wait ... it's us.
"close out the painting so people can't hide, in only a breath that was happy, then died"

Shannon Ogden,
Piscataway

I Am

I am ... thoughtful
I am ... friendly
I am ... shy
I am ... intelligent
I am ... a shadow
I am ... laughter
I am ... smiles
I am ... tears
I am ... thoughtful when I make a friend smile
I am ... friendly when I help a friend when they have tears
I am ... shy, but around my friends, I'm full of laughter
I am ... intelligent, but quiet in the classroom, so it's like I'm a shadow
Really, I am ... the pen, the paper, the poem, and most of all, myself.

Patricia Barnes,
Piscataway

I Am

I am a good thought about a book.
I am the imagination of being a rock star.
I am the thought of a bottle of Snapple that will last forever.
I am a painter's new idea.
I am a moment stuck in a photograph.
I am a drummer snapping his sticks in half.
I am a sharp edge of glass.
I am the smallest crayon in the box.
I am a moment in a book.
I am a drummer playing music that you listen to.
I am a piece of glass in the Snapple bottle.
I am the crayon used in the painting.
Really, I am whatever I can be
and what I am is what I am.

Steven Geuther,
Piscataway

I Am

I am ... light
I am ... hope
I am ... past
I am ... colorful
I am ... grass
I am ... hands
I am ... tears
I am ... pictures
I am ... a light breeze wandering through grass
I am ... hands grasping for hope that I will be found
I am ... past tears crying for help
I am ... colorful pictures being missed and looked at by family

Really I am ... a lost boy going around and trying to find his way back home.

Kenny Nguyen,
Piscataway

Summer

It's marshmallow golden,
Butterflys flutter by
Hot-sun molten
Wind chill shy

It's eight o'clock sundown
Book-reading lazy
Mother Nature's royal crown
Of daffodil and daisy

It's midsummer's night dream
Pool-jumping blue
Clouds of whipped cream
And the red robin's coo

It's vacation funtime
And the ocean's spray
The windpipe's chime
Right after May

It's August, June, July
It's Valencia orange
It's turquoise-color sky
And the creaking of a door hinge

It's cooling fan breeze
It's almost-school-bummer
It's flying honeybees
It's marshmallow golden summer!

Elena McPhillips,
Bridgewater

Baseball

The first pitch is thrown
THUMP
The ball whizzed right by the batter
The second pitch is thrown
THUMP
The batter swung and missed
He got angry
He wanted the next pitch
The 0-2 is thrown
The bat lunged at the ball
BANG
The ball flew up in the air like a plane taking off
It is high
It is far
It is GONE
HOMERUN
HOMERUN
HOMERUN
He trotted around the bases
And jumped right on Home Plate
He walked back to the dugout
With all his teammates slapping his helmet
The next batter is up
The first pitch is thrown and...

Matthew Pennella,
Martinsville

End Of The Trail
A True Story

I am dressed in all leather, while I run away.
I look down on all the people as I trot past.
When I find myself on the ground I start to
Feel a lot of pain in my shoulder. Laying
There I heard that I broke my shoulder.
I'm in a lot of pain laying here in my stall.
Trying not to move, but when I try to get up
For food and water, it hurts so much. Now
Everyone is looking at me. I'm really getting
Scared, people are bringing blankets and
Covering the stall. I'm trying to wake up,
Wishing that this is all just a dream, hoping
That I can but as hard as I try I can't, I'm not
Dreaming. As I wait to see what happens, I
Ask God why me? As I think about the whole
Day, my whole life I realize that everything
Happens for a reason, maybe if I get a
Chance to meet him he will tell me why.
As I feel a sharp pierce in my shoulder,
while my body goes numb,
I just wish I could say good bye.
As everything goes dark, I have my last few
Breaths I blink a couple times, I fall asleep...
forever.

Kim Wernerspach,
Branchburg

Songs

Sing-a-Song, Sing-a-Long
Sing-it-Right or Sing-it-Wrong
Songs are darkness
Songs are light
Songs are daytime
Songs are night
Songs are good times
Songs are bad
Songs are happy
Or songs are sad
Songs are space
Songs are earth
Songs are death
Or songs are birth
Songs are like tops
Spinning around
And the differences between them
Leave the listener astounded
Songs are known things
While others insane
Some swim like fishes
Others fly like a plane
Songs are the young
And some are the old
Songs can be sheepish
Or songs can be bold
Songs are warmth
Or songs are cold
Songs are first made up
Then they're retold
All songs are songs
And sing them you do
But the way that you sing them
Is all up to you
Sing-a-Song, Sing-along
Sing-it-Right or Sing-it-wrong

Mark Velednitsky,
Bridgewater

Chapter 9
EIGHTH GRADE

She Is In Me

She feeds me. Food.
She gives me. A bath.
She changes. My diaper.
When I was a baby.
She serves me. Food.
She takes me. To school.
When I was little.
She helps me. With homework.
When I need help.
I love her, she loves me.
She is in me.
In my heart and mind.
I'm in hers.
She is my MOM

*Rose Kasman,
Bridgewater*

My Popie

The sun still rises and sets
But our world is upset
A new hole in our hearts was dug
Everyone wants to hug
Our tears form puddles, streams and rivers
The thought of our Popie not here brings shivers.
Everyone who loved him is here today
Remembering the memories that will never
fade away
We make our love for him known
Because our old man is never coming home
Though he is still, and forever shall be here
in our spirits and our hearts.

*Jennie Frank,
Neshanic*

Before The Game

My heart pounds
Like heavy thunder
On a midnight black
Stormy night
As I step onto the field for the game
I feel butterflies in my stomach
Pinching me like yellow jackets' stingers
As I prepare to fight for our win
My body temperature rises
Making me sweat
Sweat drops the size of
Big heavy bullets
Dripping down my face
The ground making my feet feel
Like heavy dumbbells

Dragging through the muddy field
I feel the rush of adrenaline
Through my body
trying to make me weak
As I await the referee's whistle
Then suddenly the game begins
I steal the ball
Make a magnificent run
My butterflies were gone
Hey that wasn't so bad
Time to start concentrating
On a victory

Zachary Gomez,
Flemington

Metaphor, Metaphor

A metaphor is
A detailed lie
With an iota of truth to find.

To ease your mind
You remember
That bit of truth
So everything
Makes sense.
You tweak
And pull
And move the words
To form the image
You have
To show.
If you tell it
Just right,
Maybe it will make sense
To your audience,
And a keen observer
Will see you
As a crafty storyteller

W. Max Sabor,
Frenchtown

Arizona

And I will remember:
Once the road was writ upon
With silver lines
The sun blazed triumphant through the Rain
The endless loop of asphalt burning still
With heat day left behind
The rhythm of wind and rain, blood beating in warm veins,
Faded paths written faint
On the desert's sand,
Lines of silver deep-hued on blue and gray
I will remember
The way freedom blazed glorious on the horizon,
Liberty stretching, faded gray and silver,
to meet the endless sky

Sara Muehlner,
Berkeley Heights

Drowning In Her Beauty

Her intoxicating beauty
electrifies my heart,
it stuns my soul and makes
my senses fall apart. I'm
smothered by her radiance,
I'm drowning in her splendor,
her angelic face and captivating
eyes force me to surrender.
Her eyes are that of a sunset,
melting into the sea, as her and
I exchange a kiss, we can feel the
fervent emotions, heating out of control,
as we melt into each other we share one perfect
soul. I'm drowning in her beauty, I'm lost
within the waves, I'm floundered by the love
she gives me, I'll love her always.

John Neesan,
South Plainfield

My Mom

My hard-working mom,
you are the bomb.
Driving me around,
in your Chevy Astro taxi.
Whenever it can't be found,
you always get me maxi.
With or without a flower,
you always have the Power.
Yes, I may be brave,
but you are by far the bravest.
I may not be your fave,
so I'm put to the test.
Although you don't like my way,
everything will be okay.
Even if I don't want your help,

I will always need it.
You hear me when I yelp,
when I have a fit.
Happy Mother's Day
Love always,

Morgan Neas,
Flemington

Crossroads Of Life

I'd rather be part of the crew
Than in the spotlight
If privacy in my life
Was not an option

Being the center of attention,
Might lead to an illustrious life,
But being watched every minute of the day
Can turn your family into disarray.

If being the supporting cast
Will make life a little easier,
Then why not take that road
And thrive on the peacefulness life will bring you?

If fame comes your way unexpected
And ruins your existence like a disease,
Then just throw away the limelight
And choose the simple life like me.

Greg Holtzman,
Berkeley Heights

World Cup

Today I'll tell you about the World Cup
For many of you who don't know what's up
Thirty-two good teams from around the globe
Only the best will travel this hard road

Italy, Spain, Russia and the Ukraine
Brazil versus France should be a good game
But after the first round only sixteen remain
For the sixteen left it's about glory and fame

Elimination is quick and more teams are gone
The losers have left by the following dawn
For some it's a lifetime to wait four years
Older players often end up in tears

Oh my God! Did you see that crash?
Two bodies flying after the bash
The ref ran up with a yellow card in hand
One player's career finished unable to stand

G-O-A-L
This is the ultimate word spelled
Gladiators, Warriors, Supreme Athletes
For this is about the world's elite

The road to victory is a lot like war
Bodies are left all over the floor
There is no time to look behind
Eight teams are remaining for us to climb

Teams are cut in half once more
One to zero was one of the scores
Losers leaving you know are vexed
Cheering fans know the Semi's are next

Remember the colosseum and battles of old
This is a similar scene that unfolds

The stadiums have never seen such adoring fans
As the last four teams become so grand.

The passion of two more losing teams were killed
As blood, sweat and tears were spilled
A bad call by a ref some will use as an excuse
To try and appeal is of course no use

G-O-A-L
This is the ultimate word spelled
Gladiators, Warriors, Supreme Athletes
For this is about the world's elite

The FINALS are here! The Finals are here!
The last two teams for the world to cheer
Everyone get ready it's about to start
The awaited crescendo and magic foot art

At the start of this game the whistle is blown
Some spectacular plays and skill are shown
As this is the last game and there can be no doubt
One costly mistake and you are out

The winner's feeling. Can that be described?
Honor, courage but most of all pride
Thirty-one teams failed to make this spot
We're number one and we're at the top

As I bring this historic event to a close
The wine and champagne continue to flow
Celebrations and parties at some point
will end
But lifetime memories have been made for these men

G-O-A-L
This is the ultimate word spelled
Gladiators, Warriors, Supreme Athletes
For this is about the world's elite

Keith Lester,
Whitehouse Station

A Poem For Miss Louise

Above the skies
Above the sighs
Above the cries,
There you are.
Though I cannot see you.
I know you are there.
The clock ticks,
but never mind.
I love you
No matter what —
If I am in Canada
I shall miss you no less.
If I am in Greenland —
I shall love you no less.

Anna Lilley (written at age 6),
Three Bridges

The Lost Sight

As my soul mate and I walked across the sandy beach slowly,
Our thoughts and feelings changed like the winds from Winter to spring.
Sand moist as a foggy sky massaged our feet.
The sun wrapped its blanket of warmth around us.
We tip-toed toward the ocean,
Its soft yet cold spine tingling waves danced at our feet.
I am his eyes, as the sun is the light of the sky.
The heavy salty air dried our lips.
My blind soul mate, Mario, pressed his body against mine,
Making my heart flutter like the wings of a dove with water on the tops of its feathers.
Our minds slowly dimmed as the sun set off the horizon.
We walked away from the beach leaving our footprints in the wet figureless sand.
The sky filled with purple, blue and orange ... was as juicy to us as a succulent peach.

Martika Johnson,
Plainfield

Friends Forever

We've been through more than I can remember,
We met when school started in early September.
Without you, I don't know where I'd be,
My world would be too dark for me to see.
We've had our share of laughs and fights,
We've seen so many beautiful sights.
I love you more than words can explain,
People have called us crazy but we're perfectly sane!
Through the years, our friendship won't ever die,
We've watched each other smile and even cry.
No matter what, I'll always be here,
Even when you're alone with much to fear.
We're closer than I ever thought we'd be,
And I know you'll always be there for me.
You're like a sister, who's always there,
You've shown me you'll always care.
No matter what, we'll always be best friends,
Until the very end.
We promise...

Sarah Zwerko,
Raritan Borough

Filling Up With Memories

A heart full of gold
And a head full of knowledge

My grandfather is full...
Full of memories

Memories from the past
Memories from new

Family is as important as food and water
Keeping a life stable

Brotherly love ... three
Motherly care ... four

Integrity and compassion
Sincerity and sacrifice were his seal

As life went on, jobs occurred ...
Forging metal
Throwing paper
Placing wires
Flashing a badge
Hitting a ball with a bat

Completing his circle of family
Groom to a bride
Father to two miracles
And three more, but a grandfather instead

A Marine in wars
World War II
Korean

Memories of time off ...
Sitting on the beach, staring into the horizon
Plentiful splashes into pools full of not only water,

but also of caring and love
Ocean air filling our nostrils
Laughing at jokes, some not as funny as others
Walking on sidewalks and on boardwalks
Bowling
Mini golfing
Hospital and sicknesses

He is a jester
Yet a king

Resides in Randolph
With a house full of will
And memories as well

Swimming in their lake
Ice-skating on special occasions in winter

I smile when I see his golden face
Seeing past some bad times
Seeing past the beginning Alzheimer's
Seeing past the wrinkles of wisdom

My grandfather is filling
... Filling himself with memories

Lawrence Lyman (written at age 12),
Bridgewater

Imagine If

Imagine the world if it was rid of tears
Imagine if your life was rid of fears
Imagine if you could see the light
Imagine if there was no dark at night
Imagine if your dreams were full of silver and gold
Imagine if the young never truly became old
Imagine if you could live on the throne
Imagine if people weren't injury prone
Imagine if nightmares could become dreams
Imagine if things aren't as bad as they seem
Imagine if everything you had was dumped into the sea
Imagine if you weren't you, you were me
Imagine if my life was full of glory
Imagine if there wasn't a bad ending to a sad story
Imagine if you could rid the world of pain
Imagine if you couldn't find someone to blame
Imagine if perfection could be achieved without knowing
Imagine if the hatred just kept growing
Imagine if all that is left one minute,
Imagine if your life has everything in it
Imagine if you could fight the truth in your lies
Imagine if the truth in your life never dies
Imagine if you had one chance, to take it all back
Would you take what's yours, or let it slip through the crack?

Joseph Rivera,
Edison

That Bee

I was skateboarding when out of nowhere I saw a bee
On my arm I felt
A sting so painful
I looked down, there was a welt
So I said to that bee,
"I'm sure you wouldn't mind
If I took my fingers
And I pulled your behind"
He started to cringe
He started to cry
He said "how terribly rude of me
But I thought I would die
when you hit my flower
There are bee manners, I must of forgot
I promise I won't do it again
I won't sting anyone, not even a tot"
But an hour later Kyle,
Chris, Benny, and Joe
Were playing football
They were about to go
When that bee flew over
His chops he was lickin
Then he bit them in the arms
They were on the ground kickin
You could hear them screaming
You could hear them smacking
You could hear them at the top of their lungs
Going hack, hack, hacking
A bee is slick
A bee is keen
But I never, never, never
Thought a bee would be so mean

Mike Etheridge,
Glen Gardner

Battle Of Time

There we stood upon the beach
A breeze blew through our hair.
Time said, "For the future do not reach
As the future is now there."

And he pointed to the waves
Now as dark as night.
A ship over yonder paves
The past with all its might.

The past turned away, coilt,
And Time cried out in spite,
"He who wastes me art spoilt,
for moon reveals his plight!"

And the moon shone through the clouds,
And the ship ahead dissolved,
And the sunrise drove out crowds
Of the spoilt and enthralled.

Time turned round
To face the light
As we were sound
And held hands tight.

The hour was now at present
And the waves turned back to calm
As whispers said, "Resent
Not Time over yonder under palm."

There was Time beneath the tree,
A smile on his face.
"Well done, my friends," said he,
"You've spent life at good pace."

And so was ended
A tale in Rhyme,

In which Past fended
For the future and present Time.

Andrea Glauber,
Whitehouse Station

The Sky And I

Let them be as clouds
always changing, gazed, moving, compared
but always leaves your sight.
I'd rather be a bright, white moon
hangs in the sky, like the stars
sparkling above the big, wide world
To have broken through the darkness of the sun
to stand, to only show up on some days
in bits and pieces
To be covered up by clouds
carrying my friendship, my love, to where I cannot reach
or to where I cannot go
I'd rather be independent, and if
then disappeared altogether
than to be beautiful by the sun's rays
moving on by me in the dark sky
where they block, go above, and underneath me
according to the popularity
I'd rather show up during some time of the day
than being there most of the time
If I could show up in bits, being noticed or unknown
I'd rather be a bright white moon.

Kiley Thergesen,
Edison

Chapter 10
NINTH GRADE

Darkness

Darkness falls
All is gone
I stand alone
As the black covers all
The emptiness inside
Is nothing I can't hide
The solitude binds me
It keeps me inside
No light can be seen
As darkness falls
A candle burns for you
But it does not bring me light
The evil is arising
All is gone
No sound is heard
As darkness falls
And I stand alone
As the black covers all

Kayla Coady,
Hillsborough

Autumn Nights

In Autumn, the sun sets differently
than usual
The crickets chirp like a wonderful
musical
The fireflies create glowing patterns
in the sky
The birds make their last past by
In Autumn, the moon is a glowing halo
Lighting the way for a passing swallow
The leaves sway with dignity and grace
Rabbits hop from place to place
In Autumn, flowers move and sway
In the most peculiar way
Their petals dancing all night
With no care or plight
In Autumn, the night is calm and serene
And there are no people to be seen
The night belongs to the wild things
The deer run, and the owl sings
In Autumn, the sky is filled with stars
Which glow and twinkle like celestial bars
Nights in Autumn are a truly magical time
And they are mine, all mine

Anthony Savas,
Bridgewater

Blurred

Tick tock goes the sound of the
Clock that controls my life
I have as much as eight decades left to live,
But it seems as if my choices and decisions
Right
Now
Will determine my fate

How was I chosen to make these choices in my life?
Why have they come so soon?
If only the purring of my cat beside my leg
Could give me any comfort,
Then I would know
My mind is clearer to think

What happens every day seems like a blur
And even the clicking of the keyboard disturbs my thoughts
Click
Click
Clickclickclickclickclickclick

My pen and mind has become dead
More than dead
Gone
Without any sign of why
Just like the voice that sang
Many a song
That filled the room and auditorium with
Such splendor and joy
Even the thumping of my own heart cannot take me back
To the world that contained birds chirping and water crashing
Up against the sands of the Jersey Shore.

But wait ...
Do I hear a door creak open
By the bookshelf in the hallway
Is it a friend that will re-enter my life once again to
Become my muse?
Can I hear the footsteps banging against the wooden floor
Coming closer and closer?
"Who's there?"

Sarah Darish,
Whitehouse Station

Graduation Poem

There was a time not so long or far away
Where a school house stood alone on a hill
Its doors wide open, beckoning children to come inside
And they came.

They still are coming through those doors
Where new opportunities and endless possibilities lie
The times have changed and the challenges are new
But the lesson is still the same.

Pride to be who we are
Strong in our beliefs
Open to all kinds
But accepting of all the learners who have walked through these doors.

Responsibility for our actions, school work
And the path we will take.
Being on time, managing our time and
Remembering to take our time.

Goals we have dreamt of
Honor roll, leading roll, learning new languages
Reaching for the stars and going for the gold
Dreaming big, stepping up one cloud at a time.

Teamwork in our classes and on the fields
On the risers or in the stands
We learned cooperation and dedication
For a common goal

Acknowledging those who have helped us with a positive attitude
And embracing these life lessons.
Being enlightened by diversity and challenges
And meeting them with a smile.

We enter a new set of doors
But will always remember the steps that took us there.

Holding firm to our roots
Our heads will be high
And our hearts will be full
Tomorrow starts a new future!

Katelynn Snyder,
Bridgewater

Mother Is What?

She is the tissue you cry in,
She is the pillow you yell into,
She is your biggest critic,
She is your biggest fan,
She is your chauffeur,
She is an iron chef,
She is what you live for,
She is who you try to impress,
She is the first one to join your cause,
She is the one who will never desert you,
She is your personal dictator,
She is the boss of you,
She is your guardian angel,
She is your mother and your only one,
The reason I know all of this is because I am a mother's son.

Michael Canfield,
Hillsborough

Where Am I From

I'm from a place far behind the hills,
Where the two roads meet.
I'm from a place where Jay got hurt,
That one rainy morning
I'm from a place called the old school bus drop,
Where we jumped off.
I'm from a place where the sounds would only be my family, at night.
I'm from the place where all things ran free, along the stony river.
I'm from a place in the back yard where
nobody could enter, up high in the trees.
I'm from a place where the colors ran together,
Where the kids would play.
I'm from a place in the kitchen,
Where mom would be delighted with herself.
I'm from a place in the snow, where "his" keys lie,
Before he would leave us.
I'm from the memories that crossed over our minds, every time it would happen.
I'm from a place where the clue things were red,
where Jimmy could call his own.
I'm from a place unknown to be a land of everything,
Jay thought it was a land of nothing.
I'm from a place of love, he gave every moment of his life to look after me,
I love him for that, and I will never forget.

Elizabeth Varady,
Long Valley

Chapter 11
TENTH GRADE

Wednesday, 5:33 P.M.

Apt fingers that dance and maneuver
under waves of methodic synchronicity
Each member casts away its own form,
slightest to the touch, fluctuating along
the canyons; torn marble bleeds fault lines
of lightlessness, careening sideways chaotically
These bones and these joints prosper in
White-knuckled confusion, popping dryly,
Snapping in the way of dusty kindling.
The mirror is positioned on a slant
it is a pool of pristine water
the only other thing in the room
(worth mentioning)
is a bucket to hold the fish
The window fell off the wall and onto the floor
now we can finally see what's
been making all that racket
I forgot that our basement smelt
like sulfur and sand and dust
Do you remember when this was a forest?
Can you see the cave
where the bear is resting?
If you trusted me
and I asked you
would you walk down there with me?
I know it hasn't been long
me knowing you knowing me that I know you know me.
The bear is resting for the season
if we use our tip-toes
we can share the same shelter too

Jordan Galler,
Belle Mead

Untitled

Look at me what do you see?
Am I as cute as I can be?
Look into my beautiful brown eyes
That will never deceive you with lies.

How about my 5'6" height?
Do you think that I'm your type?
Do you like my bronze complexion?
Do you think the Lord has sent me as a blessing?

What about my personality?
It's pretty charming as you can see.
I'm sweet, nice, and also sincere.
I love most things and I also care.
I can sing and somewhat rap.
I write songs, poems, and I can also act.

We can start as friends, and then maybe grow closer.
When you need something to lean on,
You can use my shoulder.

If you like what I said so far,
I'll give you the key to my heart to slowly ajar.
I know we're young,
We're only teens.
You start as my prince,
Then later my king.

Kalyshia Smith,
North Plainfield

His Chair

Once was sat upon, not a spectacle
Showing a blank dark look from a distance
Sitting there, now almost a collectible
Up close, it's a mossy shade that glistens.
Occupied by a man who has now passed,
Many memories remain on its cover
Once had a voice who told stories that last
Sorrowfully bare, left to his lover.
Pain's felt with a gaze, memories linger
Forever in her heart he remains there,
Comfort when she sits, he can still bring her;
Silent conversations tell him she cares.
Even with age, it will leave her, never
Imprints fade, but their love lasts forever.

Zac Carnevale,
Glen Gardner

Without You To Hold

I lie down, pull the blanket under my chin and wrap it around myself tightly.
There's an empty space next to me where you should be. It feels like a cold
black hollowness that only you can fill.
I close my eyes. As our lips gently meet, everything inside of me suddenly comes
alive and I
know at this moment the rest of the world simply does not exist.
I want to look into your eyes and tell you how much you mean to me, how
much I need you, and how much I love you.
But as soon as I open my eyes, the spell is shattered and you are gone.

Desiree Palatino,
North Brunswick

Untitled

As I was searching without vision
You came to me one night in a dream.
You suddenly became everything that made me me.
That made me whole.
You became the calmest ocean waves coming upon the shore in a hectic place.
You were my tranquility and serenity.
You became the gust of wind pushing me further and further into places
unknown when I had no more strength. Places I was too afraid to venture alone.
You were my motivation.
An overbearing tree seeming to shade me, sheltering me from the harsh realities
of the world. You were my safe haven.
You became the sun, glaring overhead as I walked along thinking my life was
without purpose. You were my warmth. You became my guiding light.
You came to me as a reflecting pool, only my reflection wasn't only shown. Yours
appeared entwined with mine. With so many varieties of creatures surrounding
me, there was only one who stood out the most. The person who enabled me to
see. The best creature God sent to this earth. You became my equal.
My soulmate.
As I awoke I thought no more blindness. I have regained my vision.
A bright light twinkling bringing me to a vision of you.

Kevin Rivera,
Plainfield

The Game Of Life

Death — a normal pattern of life
Sure, I guess.
Yet, to lose someone so close to you
All you can ask yourself is why?
Why was it his untimely demise?
What has he done to corrupt society?
Then that saying comes into play
Life is not fair.

There's nothing to do now
No going back
What has occurred, must eventually

Be accepted
He will stay in our hearts
Although it rips me up
Tears me apart

Life is a game
Never the same
You play, it's over
You start, you lose
Why even bother?

The game of life is yet to be won
At the same time I ask myself
... has it even begun?

Nina Horowitz,
Warren

The Future

Are we prepared for the future?
A time of hard work,
A time for a new life.
Are we ready to overcome new obstacles?
Meet new people, become independent.
Stick with old friends, but also make new friends.
Can we put the past behind us?
The years of high school, the years of hard work.
To start an independent life,
No parents, no rules.
Can we take that road?
Of success, of failure.
Or will we break down from the pressure.
Of being alone, of not fitting in.
So, are you ready for that journey?

Kristen Sit,
Basking Ridge

A Loved One

The soil has given me sorrow
with the constant token of death.
The soil feels the corpses
that are placed inside its body.
The soil acknowledges sorrow
when it received drops of tears.
With many reasons why they are there
and many others that are quick to blame.
The soil feels, as it is stepped on
The soil feels, as it is dug up
The soil feels, and is covered back up.
For now the soil strengthens
when it dries
for now the soil is moist
and ready for growth.
and how the soil can help to restore
the sorrow from within.

Brian Geuther,
Piscataway

The Prize

I see a young boy struggling to be someone
He rarely smiles or has any fun
When he does, he soaks it up like the sun
Like the sun drying up rain showers
His smile will become radiant like May flowers
When he isn't working part-time hours
He's in high school
Trying hard to finish his education
And, maintain his part-time obligation
So, he won't grow up to be a slob
Walking by with his head held high
Confident in every footstep
Not falling into statistics
Because he believes he will one day
Be highly acclaimed and famed
With more respect in his name
And still be the same
Not forgetting his hard-working beginnings
Took him to his happy endings
Whether in the classroom or at work
The hard-worked sweat lingers in his shirt
And his legs and feet hurt
But he doesn't mind, because he believes
What effort he sows will reap in his benefit
And, when his boys laugh at his goals
He leaves them alone
Because negative energy breeds negative people
And he won't be that one
But he focuses on his "prize"
Until his day is done!

Selena Hamlin,
Plainfield

Chapter 12
ELEVENTH GRADE

Daddy's Girl

He was the first person she ever knew
He was the one that gave her life
It was his blood that flowed through her
He was the one that taught her
Her first steps
Her first words ...
He's been there to pick her up
Every time she fell to her knees
He'd been there to defend upon her every need
When people doubted her imagination,
He was the one to see her through
Every time she shed a tear — whether it be happy or sad
He never let each one fall
He always told her, "I got your back"
He'd never let any harm darken her doorstep...
He'd look her out, like a hawk in the midnight sky
He always told her, "I would put my very life on the line for you"
He'd look into her eyes and see
The affliction that poured out of her heart
In return she gave him nothing
Because she was the one that called him daddy ...

Aliyah King,
Plainfield

Are These Actual Miles?

She asked her dad
as she watched the galloping mile markers
race against the thick white stripes.
Is it just one road
all the way to Pittsburgh?
One line tracing this jagged mountain edge?
She turned away and began to draw
against the frozen glass.
Proud deliberate lines of kindergarten print
etched in condensation.
Etched in the rolling farm land.
She hugged her bare knees and unraveled shoe laces
to braid their fraying ends.
She sat forward to hear the Volvo's engine
that roared and started with every steep incline.
She closed her tender eyes and asked while drifting off to sleep
how much longer till we're there?
She smelled the exhaust and the rubber of tires
standing in the vacant parking lot.
He stared at her shoes, expecting response
and pulled back at his blond teenage hair
She wondered in silence.
Is it just one road all the way
to Seattle?
One line tracing this truncated end?
She turned to caress the
familiar craters of
his Chevy's red brown rusted edge
She paused and asked with a trembling voice
how long will you be gone?
He kissed her nape and tasted the gold
of her Confirmation necklace.
Not so long.
She moved away and wrapped her coat
tightly around her waist.
She wrote her name in the foggy glass
in smooth, looped cursive hand.

She wouldn't kiss him back.
He started the ignition and the loping car
rolled out into the street.
It sagged and hung from every bolt.
It wouldn't see Seattle.

Halcyon Person,
Plainfield

Hardly Picket

This fence only in her mind
Her eyes blocked from the light
The lattice covering her body holding in her soul
The shadowed x's hide her beauty
Seen through by onlookers and only blocking herself
Bruised early on before the paint started to chip before her makeup slowly flaked away
The black in her life like the shade of sky the night she fell in love
Beautiful yet eerie
Comfort is lost with each crack in the wood letting each tear seep out
Rolling from crystal blue eyes to the tanned green grass that lay beneath her
Her smile never seen the etching of rectangular boxes covers it well
Each piece laid gently, her easily breakable defense

Lauren DeVito,
Flemington

Two Hearts In One

Born in a land
Far from here,
Raised by strong hands
That protected me from fear.
Playing on the streets
And learning to be a child,
Running on my feet
While the world grew wild.
Moving to another land
Where things seemed different,
Trying to accept
All of the changes.
Growing older
And learning to be a woman,
Watching the others
Without forgetting who I am.
These worlds
Made me stronger
And my thoughts
Have grown deeper.
These countries
Have given me life,
I keep on learning
As I continue to survive.
Now I stand
Between these lands
Because two hearts in one
Is what I've become.

Francesca Figalo,
Bound Brook

Chapter 13
TWELFTH GRADE

Five Hundred Miles

I believe in downpours and the way
Your hair in spikes holds defense to the rain.
There's something so intriguing about you
That always held my attention on brisk fall nights,
Spent learning how to grow up in New Jersey.

I believe in the rain and the way
It always makes us feel alive.
There's something so stimulating about
Tiny droplets falling off our eyelashes
That made us fall to the ground with laughter,
Growing up in New Jersey.

There's something about these rainy nights,
So notable and priceless,
That have made us the closest thing to family.
You're a part of all of us, and no matter what,
You'll always be like an older brother to me.
It's been so cold here since you've left.
I've been waiting for summer's sun to hit our shoulders and keep us warm,
But it seems time is never on my side.
It's a long road home but your arrival
Will bring us all together once again.

Would it be a shame to admit
We're so used to this life of
Passing out to the sound of music in our headphones
And constantly feeling cold?
I'm used to picking up the phone to your voice,
Reassuring me that you're okay,
Five hundred miles away

Kristen Wagner,
Bridgewater

Dreaming A Rhapsody In Shades Of Despair

The bullet rips through the air like fire
Screaming in passion, hate and desire
And the sky erupts into a rose red flame
On the horizon is the promise of shame
As the steel rips my flesh, the sky fades to black
And all that I know has been wiped off the track
Erased like the future I will never know
Silenced like the scream choking in my throat
Yet the night still falls upon me like rain
And suffocates all of this loathing and pain
The drops of blood dry and die like the day
But the bullet waits as I walk away
On the street in a pool of shattered dreams
Splintered hopes killed like those frail, fragile seams
Mending my heart to the crease on my sleeve
The only strength driving my weak soul to leave
This still frame murder scene, story of my life
Where vanity died along with pain and strife
And that bullet of sorrow still weeps silently
In the night, on the street, calling to me
Wearing my blood like a warm crimson coat
Swallowing the night like the sails of a boat
And at last I can fight to look away
For the nightmare dissolves in the ashes of day

Matt Johnston,
Bridgewater

Chapter 14
NO GRADE GIVEN

Half-Way There

All is silent,
All is still,

Will we finish?
I think we will!

When all is dusky,
and all is dark,

I hear...
a husky bark!

Many miles ran,
Many miles to go!

Only 524.5 miles to go!

All is silent,
All is still,

Will we finish?
I think we will

Carmen Triola,
Westfield

Where I'm From

I am from Don Omar's meaningful words from
"Reggaeton Latino" to Frankie J's loveable lyrics of "Obsession."

I am from old family pictures taken in Chile
that I cherish with all my heart.

I am from the beautiful flag of Chile
that I represent every day.

I am from the steps outside my apartment
where my friends and I spend countless hours
Hanging out in the summer.

I am from "No me levantes la vos" (Don't raise your voice to me)
to "Entrate Nicole" (Get in Nicole.)

I am from the sweet memories of being with
my grandmother to the unforgettable times I
used to have with my truly missed grandfather.

I am from el asado y papas con mayo that my mom makes
on special occasions.

I am from the memory-filled, silver handbag my mom has
full of my childhood memories that I always look at
when I am feeling down.

Nicole Bravo,
North Plainfield

Songs Of Mother Earth

Sing to me the songs of mother earth
As soft as a breeze that whispers in my ear
Mother Earth helped create this world, she gave birth
To the trees and the nature around here
Sing to me the sounds of a river flowing
Or the pitter-patter of rain
Show me the rays of a sun glowing
Or the Strong winds of a hurricane
Show me a twister
Or a sister of three
Show me what this world is meant to be

Mary Louise Codoyannis,
Lebanon

INDEX

A
Agliata, Leah 35
Agrawal, Aneesh 4
Ahmed, Ali 3
Algoo, Jeremy 16
Almer, Christine 50
Andres, Donna 67
Antony, Sarah 49
Avery, Lisa 107

B
Bacchus, Aarifah 63
Banafato, Chris 108
Barnes, Patricia 110
Beleski, Sarah 105
Bermudez, Elena 5
Bethea, Tasha 9
Bravo, Nicole 166
Brygier, Jessi 74
Butler, Emily 36

C
Canfield, Michael 141
Carnevale, Zac 147
Carra, Nicolas 23
Cayaban, Beatrice 84
Cepparulo, Jessica 50
Chalikonda, Shalini 55
Chen, Gloria 76
Cirillo-Penn, Nolan 101
Clinton, Rachael 85
Coady, Kayla 137
Codoyannis, Mary Louise 167
Condit, Crystal 99
Coney, Jerome III 106
Crooks, Mike 82
Cullen, Genevieve 29

D
Darish, Sarah 139
Del Pozo, Leandra 99
Deonarine, Chelsea 68
DeSotelle, Emily 3

Desu, Vihar 15
DeVito, Lauren 157
Dixon, Taatiana 38
Dooley, Kathryn 45

E
Edman, Danny 9
Escott, Branden 23
Etheridge, Mike 131
Evanylo, Amy 81

F
Fedak, Haley 29
Fellin, Thomas 66
Figalo, Francesca 158
Fineman, Dana 67
Frank, Jennie 119
Fritzinger, Candi 95
Furda, Alyson 93

G
Gabbett, C.M. 75
Galler, Jordan 145
George, Robert 60
Geritano, Kirk 90
Geuther, Brian 150
Geuther, Steven 111
Glauber, Andrea 133
Goldstein, Chloe 26
Gomez, Brielle 58
Gomez, Zachary 120
Gray, Justine 29
Greenstone, Sarah 72
Greig, Connor 13
Grisales, Luisa 74
Grochowski, Stephanie 55

H
Hamlin, Selena 151
Healy, Thomas 23
Hendricks, Lauren 79
Hoey, Maureen 42
Holtzman, Greg 123

Horowitz, Nina 149
Huang, Stephanie 73

I
Ielmini, LeeAnn 95
Ierokomos, Athena 107
Ihling, Chelsea 100

J
Jedra, Christina 65
Jiminez, Ariana 100
Johnson, Jennifer 13
Johnson, Kerry 51
Johnson, Martika 126
Johnston, Matt 162

K
Kaschak, Jordan 97
Kasman, Rose 119
Keane, Tara 61
King, Aliyah 155
Klitenick, Ben 105
Koemm, Alexis 40
Koemm, Kyle 92
Kornbluth, Kimberly 46
Kowal, Anthony 75

L
Lathi, Brooke 52
Lester, Keith 125
Lilley, Anna 126
Lilly, Alexandra 16
Lucky, Najee Michael 38
Ludwigsen, Adam 33
Lyman, Lawrence 129

M
MacMath, Danielle 65
Manz, Tara 33
Mauro, Dean 57
McClain, Alisha 98
McGahan, Nick 93
McHale, Jeffrey 51

INDEX

McPhillips, Cara 48
McPhillips, Elena 112
Memoli, Danny 27
Mitchell, Quajuan 39
Muehlner, Sara 121
Murphy, Adam 21
Murray, Julia 81
Myles, Crystal 34

N
Neas, Morgan 123
Neesan, John 122
Nettler, Melanie 14
Nguyen, Kenny 111
Nichols, Kristi 22
Njoku, Yvonne Darlene 27
Northrop, Kathryn 26

O
Ogden, Shannon 110

P
Palatino, Desiree 147
Pandya, Anisha 102
Patel, Monica 77
Pennella, Matthew 113
Person, Halcyon 157
Prakash, Vivek 88
Primiero, Filippa 36
Prochko, Ryan 83

R
Reimer, Chelsea 94
Riga, Bruno 109
Riley, Matthew 109
Rivera, Joseph 130
Rivera, Kevin 148
Roseo, Lucy 104

S
Sabor, W. Max 121
Salisbury-Battista, Zachary 45
Savas, Anthony 138

Sealy, Siara 63
Seebee, Jamesetta 39
Shamsi, Zoya 103
Sharkey, Shelby 21
Sharma, Somya 87
Sikora, Julia 3
Simon, Jared 103
Sit, Kristen 149
Sitrin, Zach 96
Skowronek, Nadine 62
Smiling, Kiana 61
Smith, Kalyshia 146
Smithwick, Brandon 46
Snyder, Katelynn 141
Souksay, Jackie 101
Sparkes, Lucila 91
Specian, Andrew 105
Stein, Brandon 13
Steinberg, Ashlee 45
Stoeckel, Brandon 9
Stoyell-Mulholland, Erin 68
Sunga, Celine 78
Susko, Emily 87
Sweney, Erin Brooke 41
Szeto, Garrett 15

T
Taylor, Naomi 4
Thergesen, Kiley 133
Thompson, Ashley 35
Tichy, Anna 71
Tkach, Katy 59
Tobia, Jessica 14
Tocci, Bailey 3
Todd, Samantha 17
Towle, Samantha 98
Traina, Daniela 47
Traynor, Suanne 59
Triola, Carmen 165
Tubito, Elizabeth 64

U
Usifer, Joey 62

V
Varady, Elizabeth 142
Velednitsky, Mark 115

W
Wagner, Kristen 161
Wallace, Kevin 25
Walters, Sarah 49
Wang, Shirley 41
Ward, Veronica 89
Wernerspach, Kim 114
Whitmore, Ashley 37
Wilkinson, John 108
Woodruff, Stewart 83

Y
Yang, Annie 15
Yanza, Alvin 97
Young, Kayla 91

Z
Zwerko, Sarah 127

Printed in the United States
37277LVS00002B/430-648